word alive

-depth Small Group
ble Studies

TUDY
GUIDE

God's Glory

GOD'S GLORY

what life
is all about

Jeff Stam

FAITH
ALIVE®
Christian Resources

Grand Rapids, Michigan

Faith Alive Christian Resources published by CRC Publications.

Word Alive: In-depth Small Group Bible Studies

We welcome your comments. Call us at 1-800-333-8300 or e-mail us at
editors@FaithAliveResources.org.

ISBN 1-56212-792-6

10 9 8 7 6 5 4 3 2 1

Contents

Introduction

What is God's glory? And what does it have to do with us? In short, the answer is *God's glory has everything to do with us; it's what life is all about!*

And how do we know that? Because it's revealed to us in God's Word, the Bible. There we learn that God's glory is made known in the created universe, in God's encounters with us, and especially in Jesus Christ, God's Word incarnate.

In this Bible study, author Jeff Stam challenges us to examine what Jesus says about God's glory and what it has to do with why he came. Only then can we understand why we are created, why we are saved, and why we can share in God's glory even as we live in Christ right now in this world.

In Christ, we also grow in understanding why we face trouble in this world. Our "enemy the devil" (1 Pet. 5:8) is our Lord's "disarmed" enemy (Col. 2:15), who wants to be king. And although he's been thrown down, the devil is furious and still powerful (Rev. 12:12). So he makes war against anyone or anything that carries the scent of Christ (12:17), anything that smells powerfully of God's glory.

We need to be wary of the devil and his forces while we remain "in the world" and are "sent . . . into the world" (John 17:11, 18), but by the power of Jesus through the Holy Spirit we can be victorious. And one day our Lord will welcome us to live in God's glorious presence forever.

Till then, the question for us each day, all day, is *How well are we reflecting or revealing God's glory while we live in this world, God's world?*

May Christ through the Holy Spirit be near you and guide you as you study and learn more about God's glory.

—Paul Faber, for Faith Alive Christian Resources

Jeff Stam is a minister in the Christian Reformed Church who has served as a campus pastor, an interim pastor, a missionary in Latin America, and a managing editor for World Literature Ministries (CRC Publications). He currently serves as director of

Set Free Ministries (*www.setfreeministries.com*), a resource ministry on prayer and spiritual warfare. An accompanying leader's guide by the same author includes background material and suggestions for leading each lesson.

*What does
Jesus say about
God's glory?*

JOHN 17

Glory to God in the Highest

In a Nutshell

Our focus for this entire study, as the title suggests, will be God's glory and how it relates to our day-to-day living. In our study of John 17 we see that Jesus' focus in his ministry was the Father's glory, along with his own—a manifestation of the Father's glory. Everything Jesus did in his day-to-day living pointed to the Father. Jesus knew that nothing could add to or subtract from God's glory, but his desire was that his own glory and his disciples' (our) shared glory would point to the Father.

> Angels we have heard on high,
>   singly sweetly through the night,
> and the mountains in reply,
>   echoing their brave delight.
>
>> Gloria in excelsis Deo.
>> Gloria in excelsis Deo.
>
> Come to Bethlehem and see
>   him whose birth the angels sing;
> come, adore on bended knee
>   Christ the Lord, the newborn King.
>
>> Gloria in excelsis Deo.
>> Gloria in excelsis Deo.

—French, 18th century

John 17

¹Jesus . . . looked toward heaven and prayed:

"Father, the time has come. Glorify your Son, that your Son may glorify you. ²For you granted him authority over all people that he might give eternal life to all those you have given him. ³Now this is eternal life: that they may know you, the only true God, and Jesus Christ,

7

whom you have sent. 4I have brought you glory on earth by completing the work you gave me to do. 5And now, Father, glorify me in your presence with the glory I had with you before the world began.

6"I have revealed you to those whom you gave me out of the world. They were yours; you gave them to me and they have obeyed your word. 7Now they know that everything you have given me comes from you. 8For I gave them the words you gave me and they accepted them. They knew with certainty that I came from you, and they believed that you sent me. 9I pray for them. I am not praying for the world, but for those you have given me, for they are yours. 10All I have is yours, and all you have is mine. And glory has come to me through them. 11I will remain in the world no longer, but they are still in the world, and I am coming to you. Holy Father, protect them by the power of your name—the name you gave me—so that they may be one as we are one. 12While I was with them, I protected them and kept them safe by that name you gave me. None has been lost except the one doomed to destruction so that Scripture would be fulfilled.

13"I am coming to you now, but I say these things while I am still in the world, so that they may have the full measure of my joy within them. 14I have given them your word and the world has hated them, for they are not of the world any more than I am of the world. 15My prayer is not that you take them out of the world but that you protect them from the evil one. 16They are not of the world, even as I am not of it. 17Sanctify them by the truth; your word is truth. 18As you sent me into the world, I have sent them into the world. 19For them I sanctify myself, that they too may be truly sanctified.

20"My prayer is not for them alone. I pray also for those who will believe in me through their message, 21that all of them may be one, Father, just as you are in me and I am in you. May they also be in us so that the world may believe that you have sent me. 22I have given them the glory that you gave me, that they may be one as we are one: 23I in them and you in me. May they be brought to complete unity to let the world know that you sent me and have loved them even as you have loved me.

24"Father, I want those you have given me to be with me where I am, and to see my glory, the glory you have given me because you loved me before the creation of the world.

25"Righteous Father, though the world does not know you, I know you, and they know that you have sent me. 26I have made you known to them, and will continue to make you known in order that the love you have for me may be in them and that I myself may be in them."

What the Angels Sang

As I write the opening words for this Bible study, I find myself right in the middle of the Advent season. Carols abound—"Hark! the Herald Angels Sing," "Angels in the Realms of Glory," "Angels We Have Heard on High," and a host of others. Angels adorn nativity scenes from front lawns to storefronts. Children around the world not only try their best to act like little angels (at least some of the time), but for pageants and programs they are also dressed in angelic robes and wings, and with loud voices and happy faces they sweetly sing angel songs.

But what did the angels sing? I come up with only three main events recorded in Scripture in which angels are associated with singing. The first is mentioned in the book of Job, when God is questioning Job about where *he* was when *God* created the world. God mentions that when he "laid the earth's foundation . . . the morning stars sang together and all the angels shouted for joy" (Job 38:7). There's also the event of Jesus' birth, when angels appeared to shepherds and (apparently) sang, "Glory to God in the highest [*Gloria in excelsis Deo*]" (Luke 2:14). And in the apostle John's vision of Christ's coronation in Revelation 5 we read of "angels, numbering thousands upon thousands, and ten thousand times ten thousand," circling the throne as "they sang: 'Worthy is the Lamb, who was slain, to receive power and wealth and wisdom and strength and honor and glory and praise!'" (Rev. 5:11-12).

These songs are about God and God's *glory*. At the dawn of time angels glorified the Creator God. At the Savior's birth angels again gave glory to God, and at the same time they glorified the newborn "holy one" who would be "called the Son of God" (Luke 1:35). And when Christ began reigning as King over all creation, countless multitudes gave glory to the One "who sits on the throne and to the Lamb" (Rev. 5:13). If we remind ourselves that "all things were created . . . by [Christ] and for [Christ]" (Col. 1:16), we realize that even the singing referred to in Job refers to both God the Father and God the Son.

The Lord at Prayer

The prayer in our passage for today is often called Christ's *high-priestly prayer*. It's a beautiful example of Jesus' priestly intercession for his followers. Other than the brief lines he prayed while preaching and teaching (see Matt. 6:9-13; 11:25-26; Luke 10:21; 11:2-4; John 11:41-42; 12:28) or while he agonized in Gethsemane and on the cross, this is the only transcript we have of the Lord at prayer—and it's by far the longest. Jesus is praying for his disciples. He is praying for you and me.

Pastors and scholars often highlight Jesus' desire here for unity among his followers (17:11, 20-24) and his request that the Father watch over them while they remain in the world (17:11-12, 15). But notice that the most repeated theme in this prayer passage is God's glory. The words *glory* and *glorify* occur nine times in this prayer (five times in the preamble alone), and the emphasis on glory pervades from beginning to end, helped along by words and phrases like "revealed," "obeyed," "Holy Father," "sanctify," "let the world know," "Righteous Father," and "made you known" (17:6, 11, 17, 19, 23, 25-26).

Though we know Scripture as the inspired Word of God points out God's glory, we should take special note when Jesus, the Living Word of God, speaks about God's glory. And it's especially interesting that we are privileged to listen in on an intimate conversation Jesus is having with his heavenly Father.

The Father's Glory

Of the nine references to glory, two are direct references to the Father's glory and three are indirect. The two direct references are in John 17:1 and 17:4. Reading through the preamble of Jesus' prayer (17:1-5), we can see that the glory Jesus is referring to is the "bottom line." God's glory is not only an end result of Jesus' work; it's the overriding purpose for which Jesus came to bring eternal life. A key cause-and-effect word in 17:1 is "that" (or "so that"—NRSV). "Glorify your Son," Jesus says, "[so] *that* your Son may glorify you.*" Then Jesus goes on to say that all "the work" he has been "sent" to do for "all those" whom God has "given him" is for the Father's glory (17:2-4). In paraphrase, Jesus is saying here, *"Father, everything I have done, and the purpose for which you sent me, has been to bring you glory."* We'll dig deeper into this "bottom line" in later lessons as we take a look at passages like Ephesians 1 and as we reflect on the cosmic struggle between God and Satan.

The Son's Glory

Jesus begins his prayer by declaring that "the time has come" for him, the Son, to be glorified (17:1). It sounds almost as if Jesus is looking back on an agreement made with the Father, an agreement that had to do with glorifying Jesus if he completed the work of redemption for which he was sent. Scripture does hint at this kind of agreement, and the glory of Christ's current position "far above all rule and authority, power and dominion, and every title that can be given, not only in the present age but also in the one to come" is the reward and result of Christ's completed work (Eph. 1:21). But notice that Jesus requests this glory *so that* the Father may be glorified.

Jesus recognizes that his glory in the past, present, and future is a reflection of glory shared or held with the Father (John 17:5). Jesus' glory is something that has been given from the Father (17:22, 24), and Jesus wants his followers to see and recognize it as such. He wants all of us to see him in his true glory: "Father, I want those you have given me to be with me where I am, and to see my glory, the glory you have given me because you loved me before the creation of the world" (17:24). This is not megalomania on Jesus' part; his glory is not delusional but real. Jesus is really God, and he wants his disciples, his followers, his "friends" (15:13-15), to know him completely, glory and all, and to see him in relationship with the Father, glory and all.

Our Glory

Toward the end of his prayer Jesus says, "I have given them the glory that you gave me, that they may be one as we are one: I in them and you in me" (17:22-23). This is incredible! We, too, share in this glory that Jesus is talking about. Christ shares it with us so that we can be one with him and with each other, so that we can experience the oneness that the Son has with the Father (and the Holy Spirit). And just as Christ has received glory with the purpose of further glorifying the Father, so we have received glory to reflect the glory of God the Father and the Son (and the Holy Spirit)—by being one like they are and being one with them. Through the power of the Spirit working in us, this becomes more and more natural as our oneness with the triune God takes shape and guides our living (2 Cor. 3:18).

GENERAL DISCUSSION

1. What are the most common themes in the songs you usually sing as part of worship? How many of them are about God's glory? Do you sing songs in your personal worship? If so, what do you most often sing about?

2. How would you distinguish between praise and glory? How are they associated? In what ways have you praised God today or in the past week?

3. As you read through Jesus' prayer in John 17, what do you find most striking? Why? Do you find it directly applicable to your daily living? If so, how?

4. What work has God given you to complete? Does it give glory to God? Explain.

5. In what ways has Jesus given you glory? How is it evidenced in your life? Does it feel like a daily reality for you? Why or why not?

SMALL GROUP SESSION IDEAS

Opening (5-10 minutes)

Pray—As soon as everyone is situated, open your session with prayer. It would be best to do this before introductions and sharing of other information. Giving priority to prayer this way will help you as a group to avoid chit-chat that can tend to edge into your prayer and study time. The opening prayer can be a brief one for blessing and guidance as you begin your study of God's glory together. Recognize God's presence and the seriousness of your subject matter. Humbly and yet boldly ask God's Spirit to teach and touch each one of you.

Introductions—During this first session you may want to spend some time on introductions of both people and material. For starters, each one of you could share some general information about yourself, such as your name and occupation (or church affiliation, if you come together from various churches).

Take a few minutes also to get acquainted with the study material, if you haven't already done so. A quick way to do this would be to review the table of contents and the section titled "In a Nutshell" at the beginning of this lesson.

You may also want to take a few minutes to talk about your expectations as you begin this study. As an opening exercise, come up with a group definition of *God's glory* (then you could compare your ideas with other responses you might come up with later when you do General Discussion question 2).

Going Through the Material (15-20 minutes)

You can use several dynamics for going through the study material. For example, even if everyone has read the Scripture ahead of time, reading it again together can serve as a helpful review. Reading or reviewing sections of the study notes can also be helpful, depending on how much time you have. The Scripture for this lesson has three natural divisions—Jesus' prayer for himself (John 17:1-5), for his disciples (17:6-19), and for future believers (17:20-26)—so it's easily divided among three readers. And this lesson's commentary is presented in five short sections, so it can be divided among five readers or reviewers, if you like.

Another thing you might like to try from time to time is to share comments or questions on any particular section that's been read or reviewed. Then you can jot down ideas and questions that you may want to pursue later during your discussion.

Discussing the Material (25-30 minutes)

Most groups will find there are more than enough questions to generate discussion. If you don't know each other well, your trust and self-confidence in sharing thoughts and ideas, including personal information and experiences, may not be very strong, but it will tend to grow as you get to know each other better.

Many of the General Discussion questions encourage personal application. Some of these may require quite a bit of thought, so feel free to take some time to reflect before giving your responses. Of course, if you're not comfortable with sharing about personal experiences, you shouldn't feel pressured to.

Till Next Time (5 minutes)

This section presents goalsetting options aimed at putting ideas into action. You are free, of course, to change the ideas here to fit your particular needs or preferences, or you can supply entirely different ideas if you want to. During later sessions it will also be important to follow up on your progress with the goals you've set.

- Choose one thing in your daily work or other activities that you can use as an instrument to glorify God. Find someone with whom you can share your thoughts about this. After a week, share with that person how things are going in relation to the choice you've made.

- In the coming week take some time each day to read and meditate on 2 Thessalonians 2:13-14. Reflect on how this truth can influence your daily living.

Closing (5-10 minutes)

If you have time, do some sharing about prayer needs, especially in connection with the lesson material. If you have purposefully decided to include personal and other needs, feel free to do more in-depth sharing.

Then close with prayer. Depending on time and how you interact as a group, you could have everyone offer sentence prayers, or you could perhaps have one person pray.

If you like to sing, you can also sing together the song used to introduce the lesson material, or you could choose another song that fits well with the material.

What's it like to experience God's glory?

EXODUS 14:4, 15-18; 15:1-5, 11; 24:15-18; 33:12-23; 34:5-10, 29-35; 40:34-38

Experiencing God's Glory

In a Nutshell

In the Old Testament, God's glory was often closely related to the presence of God. In this lesson we look at ways in which God made his presence and glory unmistakable not only to Israel but to all other peoples as well.

Moses and the Israelites sang this song to the LORD:

"I will sing to the LORD,
　for he is highly exalted.
The horse and its rider
　he has hurled into the sea.
The LORD is my strength and my song;
　he has become my salvation.
He is my God, and I will praise him,
　my father's God, and I will exalt him.
The LORD is a warrior;
　the LORD is his name.
Pharaoh's chariots and his army
　he has hurled into the sea.
The best of Pharaoh's officers
　are drowned in the Red Sea.
The deep waters have covered them;
　they sank to the depths like a stone. . . .

"Who among the gods is like you, O LORD?
　Who is like you—
　　majestic in holiness,
　　awesome in glory,
　　working wonders?"

—Exodus 15:1-5, 11

Exodus 14:4, 15-18

4". . . I will harden Pharaoh's heart, and he will pursue them. But I will gain glory for myself through Pharaoh and all his army, and the Egyptians will know that I am the LORD." . . .

15Then the LORD said to Moses, "Why are you crying out to me? Tell the Israelites to move on. 16Raise your staff and stretch out your hand over the sea to divide the water so that the Israelites can go through the sea on dry ground. 17I will harden the hearts of the Egyptians so that they will go in after them. And I will gain glory through Pharaoh and all his army, through his chariots and his horsemen. 18The Egyptians will know that I am the LORD when I gain glory through Pharaoh. . . ."

24:15-18

15When Moses went up on the mountain, the cloud covered it, 16and the glory of the LORD settled on Mount Sinai. For six days the cloud covered the mountain, and on the seventh day the LORD called to Moses from within the cloud. 17To the Israelites the glory of the LORD looked like a consuming fire on top of the mountain. 18Then Moses entered the cloud as he went on up the mountain. And he stayed on the mountain forty days and forty nights.

33:12-23

12Moses said to the LORD, "You have been telling me, 'Lead these people,' but you have not let me know whom you will send with me. You have said, 'I know you by name and you have found favor with me.' 13If you are pleased with me, teach me your ways so I may know you and continue to find favor with you. Remember that this nation is your people."

14The LORD replied, "My Presence will go with you, and I will give you rest."

15Then Moses said to him, "If your Presence does not go with us, do not send us up from here. 16How will anyone know that you are pleased with me and with your people unless you go with us? What else will distinguish me and your people from all the other people on the face of the earth?"

17And the LORD said to Moses, "I will do the very thing you have asked, because I am pleased with you and I know you by name."

18Then Moses said, "Now show me your glory."

19And the LORD said, "I will cause all my goodness to pass in front of you, and I will proclaim my name, the LORD, in your presence. I will have mercy on whom I will have mercy, and I will have compassion on whom I will have compassion. 20But," he said, "you cannot see my face, for no one may see me and live."

21Then the LORD said, "There is a place near me where you may stand on a rock. 22When my glory passes by, I will put you in a cleft in the rock and cover you with my hand until I have passed by. 23Then I will remove my hand and you will see my back; but my face must not be seen."

34:5-10, 29-35

5Then the LORD came down in the cloud and stood there . . . and proclaimed his name, the LORD. 6And he passed in front of Moses, proclaiming, "The LORD, the LORD, the compassionate and gracious God, slow to anger, abounding in love and faithfulness, 7maintaining love to thousands, and forgiving wickedness, rebellion and sin. Yet he does not leave the guilty unpunished; he punishes the children and their children for the sin of the fathers to the third and fourth generation."

8Moses bowed to the ground at once and worshiped. 9"O Lord, if I have found favor in your eyes," he said, "then let the Lord go with us. Although this is a stiffnecked people, forgive our wickedness and our sin, and take us as your inheritance."

10Then the LORD said: "I am making a covenant with you. Before all your people I will do wonders never before done in any nation in all the world. The people you live among will see how awesome is the work that I, the LORD, will do for you." . . .

29When Moses came down from Mount Sinai with the two tablets of the Testimony in his hands, he was not aware that his face was radiant because he had spoken with the LORD. 30When Aaron and all the Israelites saw Moses, his face was radiant, and they were afraid to come near him. ³¹But Moses called to them; so Aaron and all the leaders of the community came back to him, and he spoke to them. ³²Afterward all the Israelites came near him, and he gave them all the commands the LORD had given him on Mount Sinai.

³³When Moses finished speaking to them, he put a veil over his face. ³⁴But whenever he entered the Lord's presence to speak with him, he removed the veil until he came out. And when he came out and told the Israelites what he had been commanded, ³⁵they saw that his face was radiant. Then Moses would put the veil back over his face until he went in to speak with the LORD.

40:34-38

³⁴Then the cloud covered the Tent of Meeting, and the glory of the LORD filled the tabernacle. ³⁵Moses could not enter the Tent of Meeting because the cloud had settled upon it, and the glory of the LORD filled the tabernacle.

³⁶In all the travels of the Israelites, whenever the cloud lifted from above the tabernacle, they would set out; ³⁷but if the cloud did not lift, they did not set out—until the day it lifted. ³⁸So the cloud of the LORD was over the tabernacle by day, and fire was in the cloud by night, in the sight of all the house of Israel during all their travels.

What the Israelites Sang

In lesson 1 we reflected on the song the angels sang when Jesus was born. It was a celebration; it was an announcement. The song in Exodus 15, often referred to as the song of Moses and Miriam, was also a celebration and an announcement. It was a celebration of *escape from* and *victory over* Pharaoh and his army. In graphic detail it describes the hurling of war horse and rider into the sea (Ex. 15:1).

The announcement of this song is a proclamation of God's glory (15:2, 11):

> "The LORD is my strength and my song;
>   he has become my salvation.
> He is my God, and I will praise him. . . .

> "Who among the gods is like you, O LORD?
>   Who is like you—
>   majestic in holiness,
>   awesome in glory,
>   working wonders?"

In just a few lines this rhetorical question in Exodus 15 says it all: there are *no* gods like "the LORD." Our God works wonders, showing in no uncertain terms that the true Lord over Israel, over Egypt, over all this world is "awesome in glory."

And how do God's people respond to glory confirmed in such an awesome way? The Israelites sang and danced!

Defining Glory

In lesson 1 we also thought about how we might define God's glory. That's a much more difficult task than we might have thought at first.

Frankly, I have to say that this study has been one of the most intimidating tasks I have ever set a pen to. I'd been thinking about glory and how it might make for an interesting study, but when I actually began trying to write a study on God's glory, I soon felt as though I were being far too daring. The task became intimidating, and I felt minuscule in comparison to the awesome glory of God.

Let me say at the outset that God's glory will not be put in a box. It cannot be stuffed inside the covers of a book or booklet. We will not be able to fully understand it, envision it, or even imagine it—not to mention our inability to encapsulate it in a definition made with the limitations of human language. Is the concept of God's glory a noun? Yes. Is it an adjective? Yes—and superlative at that. Is it a verb? Yes.

I've heard the following apologetic for the concept of faith: "Faith is like love. You can't touch it, measure it, or satisfactorily describe it, but that makes it no less real. You must experience it to begin to understand it. It cannot be taught." I suppose the same can be said of God's glory—though to a far greater degree. We can "experience" God's glory in different ways, as did Moses and the Israelites, but even then we can only know it from a distance. It is simply too great for us.

Gaining Glory

It's interesting to note that Exodus 14:4 is the first passage in the Old Testament to mention God's glory. We don't see God's glory mentioned in the creation account or in the destruction account (the flood). Scripture doesn't mention that God revealed his glory to Abraham, Isaac, or Jacob. Even in Exodus 3:1-5, where we read that Moses stood on holy ground before a burning bush, there is no reference to God's glory. I think it can be argued that God's glory was evidenced in creation, and it is highly likely that the patriarchs experienced something of the glory of God in their dealings and experiences with the Lord. The scriptural narrative, however, does not point out God's glory until the people of God are cornered—with the Red Sea in front of them and Pharaoh's army closing in from behind. In fact, 14:4 shows us that this cornering was God's design. The Lord had a plan: "I will gain glory for myself."

God adjusted circumstances and attitudes (14:17) for the purpose of gaining glory. And that, in turn, served the purpose of making God known as "the LORD" (14:4, 18). Notice that while God's glory is at the center here, it also serves to bring God greater glory by making God better known. The continuing, progressive revelation of God's glory serves to glorify God more and more. In this case God revealed his identity not only to Israel but also to the Egyptians and to all others who would recognize God for who he truly is.

Experiencing Glory

While we may deeply desire to experience God's glory, the experience may be more awesome and terrifying than we can imagine. When Moses went up on Mount Sinai, "the cloud" settled on the mountain, literally covering it (24:15). This appears to be the same cloud we read about in Exodus 19 in the context of God's preparing Moses and the people to receive the law. The account in Exodus 24 parallels and follows up on the account in Exodus 19, adding other important details (see also 20:18-21). With or in this cloud came "the glory of the LORD" (24:16; see 19:9), so the Israelites were able to experience God's glory in terms of a physical manifestation, something they could see. To describe what they saw, the narrator writes that it "looked like a consuming fire" (24:17; see 19:18). For them, God's glory was something both majestic and terrifying (see 20:18-21). Is the glory of God a fire? Most likely not, but that's how God presented it to the people of Israel. (See Deut. 4:24 and Heb. 12:29 for similar imagery describing God as "a consuming fire.")

Moses experienced God's glory differently. He was invited into the cloud while all the other Israelites were commanded to stay back or be put to death (24:18; see 19:12-13). We're not told if Moses had the same fiery perception of God's glory, but we are told that he remained enveloped by that cloud, surrounded by the Lord's presence, for forty days. During that time God revealed more about his identity and glory through the wonder of his law. It would be the vehicle for holiness so that the people could be for God "a kingdom of priests and a holy nation" (19:6; see 1 Pet. 2:9; Rev. 1:6; 5:10). (See also the account of God's meeting with Moses, a few priests, and the seventy elders of Israel in Ex. 24:1-2, 9-11. Here God is described in other physical terms, welcoming them to a feast.)

Despite their experience of God's glory, the Israelites became impatient. They were not able to see past the consuming fire, so they assumed Moses had perished in the cloud. It seems they decided that this God was too terrible, so they chose lesser gods, represented by a golden calf without glory (32:1-4). That event caused Moses to ask God for permission to go deeper, to know something more of God (33:13).

Moses was aware of God's presence, and he knew that in some way God's glory was associated with God's presence. But he also knew there was more, and he wanted to experience more. When God promised, "My Presence will go with you," to show all the world that the Lord was with Moses and Israel (33:14, 16), Moses pressed further, saying, "Now show me your glory" (33:18). Moses wanted to *see* God's glory. God then said, "I will cause all my goodness to pass in front of you, and I will proclaim my name, the LORD, in your presence" (33:19). But the Lord also explained that Moses would not be able to bear the fullness of God's glory: "You cannot see my face, for no one may see me and live" (33:20).

It was probably impossible for Moses to adequately describe the experience of having God's glory pass by and seeing God's "back" (33:23), but the encounter was obvious. The experience of God's glory made Moses' face radiant—so much so that the people feared him when they saw him afterward. Because of this, Moses veiled the remaining glow of God's glory until he went into the Lord's presence again (34:29-35).

Following God's Glory

God's *shekinah* glory filled "the Tent of Meeting," the "tabernacle" (40:34), as the Lord had promised Moses (29:43). Again, this glory was visibly evidenced by the cloud, which contained fire at night (40:38). The cloud represented God's presence. Whenever the cloud moved, it meant God was moving—or, more precisely, that God was leading and Israel was to follow (40:36-37; see 13:21-22). For the nation of Israel, the presence of God implied that God's glory was with them. And they followed it wherever it went. The Israelites were not simply chasing clouds; they were pursuing God's glory.

The pursuit of God's glory is *what life is all about.* We, like Israel, are called to be God's "treasured possession": "a kingdom of priests and a holy nation" (Ex. 19:5-6). We are called to pursue God's glory by living in holiness in relationship with the Lord. God is present with us, and we are called to watch and listen in faith in order to follow God's leading. In these ways God is glorified and we share in God's glory.

GENERAL DISCUSSION:

1. In what ways has the glory of God been confirmed in your life? Think of one or two examples. In what ways have you responded to these evidences of glory?

2. Can you think of specific instances in your life or in others' lives in which God has adjusted circumstances or attitudes for his purposes? How about in your church or study group? In what ways did those situations give glory to God?

3. In what ways would you (or do you) picture God's glory?

4. Have you ever felt enveloped by God's glory? If so, what were the circumstances, and what was the experience like?

5. In what ways have you followed God's glory in the past week or so? What can you do in the coming week to be more aware of where God's glory is leading you?

SMALL GROUP SESSION IDEAS

Opening (5-10 minutes)

Pray/Worship—As you open with prayer for this session, ask God's Spirit to help each of you focus on experiencing God's glory while you study Scripture together. A reading from the song of Moses and Miriam (printed at the beginning of the lesson material) may work well as an opening worship element at this time.

Follow-up from previous session—If you used the goalsetting option(s) from lesson 1, include some time for follow-up during this session.

Introductions—If any newcomers are with you for this session, go through a brief round of introductions, as you may have done during the previous session.

Your leader may also take a few minutes to introduce the lesson material.

Going Through the Material (15-20 minutes)

The material for this session includes several Scripture passages. If you like to read the Scriptures during your session time, you may want to read sections as they correspond with comments in the study-guide notes for this session. The passages from Exodus 14 correspond with the section on "Gaining Glory"; the passages from chapters 24 and 33-34 correspond with "Experiencing Glory"; and the passage from chapter 40 corresponds with "Following God's Glory."

Discussing the Material (25-30 minutes)

In this lesson some of the discussion questions are closely related in content, so you may notice some overlap among them. That's okay. The intention is to keep focusing on experiencing God's glory so that everyone has plenty of opportunity to reflect on and share thoughts about this topic.

In response to question 3, you may want to illustrate your visualizations of God's glory. See what you can do, for example, with a few markers, crayons, and paper. Another option may be to use overhead transparencies so that you can project your illustrations.

If your "comfort zone" and time allow, you may also wish to engage in some deeper sharing. Perhaps someone would like to mention a calling that God has laid on his or her heart, a (re)commitment, or even a confession.

Till Next Time (5 minutes)

Try one or more of the following goalsetting options during the coming week:

- Reflect on the relationship between God's glory and God's presence. An important term in this regard is *shekinah,* a transliteration of the Hebrew term meaning "that which dwells." *Shekinah* is not a biblical term but is "used in many of the [rabbinical] Jewish writings to speak of God's presence. The term . . . is implied throughout the Bible whenever it refers to God's nearness either in a person, object, or his glory. It is often used in combination with glory to speak of the presence of God's *shekinah* glory" (*Holman Bible Dictionary*).

- Compare the promises in Exodus 19:5-6 with those in 1 Peter 2:9-10. Reflect on how these passages are similar and different. Think about what each has to do with God's glory and how we live our lives.

- Do a comparison study of Exodus 40, about God's glory coming into the Tent of Meeting (tabernacle), and Ezekiel 10, about God's glory departing from the temple. Note the similarities and differences between the two events, including the circumstances surrounding them. Then note the similarities and differences between those events and God's presence in the church today.

Closing (5-10 minutes)

Close with prayer. As was noted in the previous session, if you have time, do some sharing about prayer needs, especially in connection with the lesson material. Ask the Lord to help each of you stay focused throughout the coming week on experiencing God's glory.

If you like to sing, you might try a musical version of Moses and Miriam's song from Exodus 15, or you could sing another meaningful song that focuses on God's glory.

Another option would be to read Psalm 34 together. This psalm ties in beautifully with several of the themes and issues discussed in the material for this session.

There's more to
creation than
meets the eye.

God's Glory in Creation

In a Nutshell

In lesson 2 we spoke of God's glory related to God's presence. Now let's look at God's glory reflected in creation, musing mainly on Psalm 19. When David prepared this declaration of God's glory for the choir, he was limited to what the unaided eye could see. Today, although we face the obstacles of smog and city-light pollution, we also have the advantage of space-based telescopes that show us far more than David could have imagined.

> This is my Father's world,
> and to my listening ears
> all nature sings and round me rings
> the music of the spheres.
> This is my Father's world;
> I rest me in the thought
> of rocks and trees, of skies and seas—
> his hand the wonders wrought.
>
> —Maltbie D. Babcock, 1901, alt.

Psalm 19:1-6

¹The heavens declare the glory of God;
the skies proclaim the work of his hands.
²Day after day they pour forth speech;
night after night they display knowledge.
³There is no speech or language where their voice is not heard.
⁴Their voice goes out into all the earth,
their words to the ends of the world.

In the heavens he has pitched a tent for the sun,
⁵ which is like a bridegroom coming forth from his pavilion,
like a champion rejoicing to run his course.
⁶It rises at one end of the heavens
and makes its circuit to the other;
nothing is hidden from its heat.

Romans 8:18-21

¹⁸ I consider that our present sufferings are not worth comparing with the glory that

25

will be revealed in us. [19]The creation waits in eager expectation for the sons of God to be revealed. [20]For the creation was subjected to frustration, not by its own choice, but by the will of the one who subjected it, in hope [21]that the creation itself will be liberated from its bondage to decay and brought into the glorious freedom of the children of God.

Listening to Creation

Most of us have had the experience of being simply awestruck at the beauty, power, or complexity of creation. I've had this experience many times. Growing up on Lake Michigan, I enjoyed going down to the piers and watching storms come in. The combination of thunder, lightning, and huge breakers gives an inspiring show.

I've also been fortunate enough to see the aurora borealis (northern lights) a couple of times. A few years ago my wife, Denise, and I went whale watching off the New England coast. And when we lived in Washington for two years, we had a daily picture-window view of Mount Rainier.

I was present at the births of both of my children, so I had the privilege of watching new life come forth. Even in the midst of big cities I've been awed at what people can build with the abilities God has created in them. And just the marvel of what's involved in taking a jump shot and swishing a basketball through a hoop twenty-five feet away boggles the mind.

These experiences and thousands more in everyday life are the speech of creation. They all "declare the glory of God" (Ps. 19:1). When I'm driving through mountains, it's hard for me to stay focused on the road because I'm so intent on watching God's creation—that is, listening to it "proclaim the work of his hands" (19:1). But I suppose that people who live in such beautiful places all their lives get used to it—at least to some extent. The marvelous speech of creation that we are regularly exposed to can tend to become little more than background noise—always there but less and less noticed. How can we become and remain active participants in creation's intended purpose of giving God glory?

The Heavens Declare

Try to visualize what David the psalmist is expressing in Psalm 19. His intent is to transform his impressions into song. David draws on his experiences of observing the heavens. Maybe he's looking back to his nights as a shepherd boy, passing the long hours observing the stars and playing his harp. Or perhaps he's recalling his many nights camped as a soldier, a commander spending a couple hours in solitude before the dawn brings battle. In any case, the psalmist is describing what he has seen (heard). To David, the constancy of the stars and the rising and setting of the sun not only point to God; they also shout out God's glory, beckoning to all who see (and hear): "Look and enjoy a glimpse of the glory of God!"

Last year my wife and I were in Mali, West Africa. There, on the southern edge of the Sahara Desert, we saw stars as we've never seen them before. It was probably the closest we'd ever come to seeing what Abraham saw when God challenged him: "Look up at the heavens and count the stars—if indeed you can count them" (Gen. 15:5). With no interference of artificial light at night or smog by day, the display of the stars and of the sun that "rises at one end of the heavens and makes its circuit to the other," with nothing "hidden from its heat," takes on new meaning. The question that continues to stump secular science as it observes the universe around us, especially the stars and planets, is that of grand design. When we look at creation as David did and we listen as David did, we see and hear clearly that creation is far too glorious to be anything other than the handiwork of a glorious God.

Glorious Freedom

In Romans 8 the apostle Paul takes a slightly different tack. Paul doesn't speak of the glory that creation declares; instead he depicts creation as looking ahead with "eager expectation" to a renewing of the glory it once knew. The passage in which we read these words (Rom. 8:18-21) is focusing on the universal effects of sin and on all creation's longing for the day when the bondage of sin, decay, and death will be broken. Not only was the image of God in humankind horribly deformed through sin, but creation was also "subjected to frustration" and "bondage to decay" (8:20-21). Paul could see all this already two thousand years ago—how would he describe the blemish on creation today?!

Paul speaks of creation being "liberated from its bondage" and "brought into . . . freedom"—and he's referring to the same "glorious freedom" we are redeemed to experience as "the children of God" (8:21). What should we make of this?

Some people would argue that creation and all of nature is not only a living organism but has "soul/spirit" qualities, allowing it to be sensitive to feeling, emotion, and "personal" interaction. This is a pantheistic view of creation, suggesting that all parts of it—plants, animals, minerals, and more—are merely different facets of God. This view teaches that there's a spiritual oneness in all things and that all things must therefore coexist in peace and harmony. Freedom for creation, according to pantheism, means that humanity does not use creation but exists with it, claiming no greater or lesser importance. This view has taken on a variety of twists throughout human history, and today in our own culture, along with other principles of Eastern mysticism mixed with animism and Western naturalism and individualism, it is present in a worldview we call New Age.

The Word of God, however, tells us that "the creation waits in eager expectation for the sons of God to be revealed" (8:19). What will be revealed is the renewing of our imagebearing status. God offers to share his glory (as we noted in lesson 1) so that we may be bearers of glory. Creation is subordinate to and waiting on humankind, and Paul, using the language of personification, points to a day when all creation will also be remade. Creation will be restored to its original state as a perfect proclaimer of God's glory.

Caring for Creation

We have many good reasons to care properly for creation. If we want to enjoy it aesthetically, we need to protect its beauty. If we want to benefit from plants and animals and oceans and ores, we need to make sure we don't abuse the earth's natural resources. If we want to protect a well-balanced ecosystem, we need to be environmentally concerned. These are some of the practical, utilitarian reasons for caring for creation.

Ideally, as God's imagebearers, we are commanded to watch over the earth and all that God has placed under our supervision. The command in itself should make us careful. The primary reason, though, for being diligent in our care and responsibility for creation is that the natural world gives glory to God. Everything we do or allow that harms creation or the created order dulls or mutes its expression of God's glory. Creation is like a mirror intended to reflect the glory of God, and humanity has often carelessly smudged and tarnished that mirror.

Errors

When we observe the greatness of creation, we must take care also to avoid a great error. God cautions us against the worship of any created thing. The human tendency to worship things in nature has been recorded in the history of almost every culture, and God speaks clearly against it (Ex. 20:4, 5). One of the saddest texts in Scripture relates to this error: "They exchanged the truth of God for a lie, and worshiped and served created things rather than the Creator" (Rom. 1:25).

In some ways environmentalism can be a twisted form of false worship. Almost every group or movement influenced by New Age thinking tends to be highly involved in environmental issues. This involvement, sadly, is not from recognizing creation as a reflection of God's glory. It's related to the mistaken pantheistic concept that all of creation is God and that "Godness" is found in all created things. Often the wonderful-sounding call to unity and peace as people come together to celebrate nature and earth is merely an invitation to join together in misplaced worship of the created rather than the Creator. This robs God of glory.

GENERAL DISCUSSION

1. The Hebrew word translated as "glory" in Psalm 19:1 literally means "weightiness" in terms of *bulk* and *abundance* and, in the abstract, in terms of *honor* and *greatness*. When you think along these lines, what are some of the ways you see or sense God's "weightiness" in creation?

2. As a group, make a list of the most phenomenal things you have ever seen. In what ways did they testify to God's glory? At the time, did you respond by giving glory to God? In what ways? Why?

3. Give some contemporary examples of how honoring something God has made has turned to improper worship.

4. What are some practical ways in which we can honor creation as a vehicle intended to glorify God, without falling into errors?

SMALL GROUP SESSION IDEAS

Opening (5-10 minutes)

Pray/Worship—Open your session with prayer, asking the Lord to help each one of you reflect in creative, thoughtful ways about the universe God has made—and why. Ask also for the Spirit's guidance and wisdom as you discuss this lesson material together.

If you like singing together, you could use the song printed at the beginning of the study-guide notes for this session: "This Is My Father's World." Or you could try another song that celebrates God's glory and power in creation, such as "How Great Thou Art," "All Things Bright and Beautiful," "We Bow Down," or "Shout to the Lord." You could also read or sing Psalm 104, which helps us focus on praising and glorifying God as the earth's creator and sustainer.

Follow-up from previous sessions—Take a few minutes to follow up on the Till Next Time goals you may have committed to during previous sessions.

Introductions—If any newcomers are with you for this session, be sure to include a brief round of introductions, as you may have done during previous sessions.

Your leader may also take a few minutes to introduce the material, as suggested in previous sessions.

Going Through the Material (15-20 minutes)

If you'd like to read the Scripture passages for this lesson before beginning your discussion, perhaps everyone could participate this time, with each person reading a sentence. This way each one of you can take part in celebrating the glory of God declared in these passages. You may also wish to read or review sections of the study-guide notes.

Discussing the Material (25-30 minutes)

If you have time, try to cover each one of the General Discussion questions for this lesson.

Till Next Time (5 minutes)

Here are some goalsetting options you could try as follow-up exercises to this lesson (or you may wish to try some ideas of your own):

- Watch a sunrise or sunset and write a psalm to God based on the experience. Think about how you can share your experience or your psalm with someone, or perhaps with your group during another study session.

- On a clear night spend some time lying on your back and gazing up at the starry sky. Try tallying stars until you lose count. Think about the splendor of each point of light in the sky, how far away it is, how long it's been there, how the Lord gave it its place in the heavens. Look for movement— you may be able to glimpse a shooting star (meteorite), a satellite, a space shuttle, or a jet coursing across the sky. Think about the awesome God who made the expansive heavens and yet gave tiny humankind the ability to soar into them. Talk to God as long as you want to, knowing that he always listens. Reflect on how you can grow in glorifying God in your life. Think about a way you can share your impressions with someone or with your group during another study session.

Closing (5-10 minutes)

Close by sharing prayer concerns and praises and approaching the Lord in prayer. Thank God for the beautiful creation, of which each one of us is a part. Praise God for sending Jesus Christ to save us from sin and to make it possible for us to live as new creatures who look forward to everlasting life in God's presence on the new earth someday. Everyone may join in with praises and petitions. Also ask the Lord to help each of you stay focused on experiencing God's glory throughout the coming week. A reading of Psalm 8, either by one person or in unison, would make a fitting ending to your prayer.

Group Project on Stewardship (Optional)

For a project that can help you get into caring for God's creation, you might consider doing some cleanup work (as in a local Adopt-a-Highway or Adopt-a-Stream program) or recycling (helping with a paper drive or glass drive or with Christmas-tree chipping) in your own community; spreading the word among church members and throughout your community about our obligation to care for the earth; or simply learning more about responsible stewardship of the earth in our society today. A helpful resource on this topic is Calvin B. DeWitt's *Earth-Wise: A Biblical Response to Environmental Issues* (CRC Publications, 1994), a study that includes discussion questions for use in group settings.

Group Study Project (Optional)

Some or all of you may be interested in studying about New Age teachings from a Reformed perspective. A helpful book on this topic, with study questions at the end of each chapter, is *Where Do We Draw the Line?: The Seductive Power of New Age* (CRC Publications, 1996) by J. William Smit.

What are God's intentions for us anyway?

4

1 CORINTHIANS 10:31; EPHESIANS 1:3-6, 11-14

Why We Are Made and Redeemed

In a Nutshell

God's glory isn't just a natural by-product of creation. God was glorious in majesty and splendor before creating anything. And yet God did create, and God's intention in doing so was to be glorified. In this lesson, as we look at God's redeeming us in Christ, we (re)discover that God's intentions for us go further and deeper than we might tend to think.

> For thou, O Lord, art high above all the earth;
> Thou art exalted far above all gods.
>
> I exalt thee, I exalt thee, I exalt thee, O Lord.
> I exalt thee, I exalt thee, I exalt thee, O Lord.
>
> —Pete Sanchez, Jr.; 4723 Hickory Downs, Houston, TX 77084. From *Songs for Praise and Worship* (Word Publishing). All rights reserved. Used by permission.

1 Corinthians 10:31

Whether you eat or drink or whatever you do, do it all for the glory of God.

Ephesians 1:3-6, 11-14

3Praise be to the God and Father of our Lord Jesus Christ, who has blessed us in the heavenly realms with every spiritual blessing in Christ. 4For he chose us in him before the creation of the world to be holy and blameless in his sight. In love 5he predestined us to be adopted as his sons through Jesus Christ, in accordance with his pleasure and will—6to the praise of his glorious grace, which he has freely given us in the One he loves. . . .

11In him we were also chosen, having been predestined according to the plan of him who works out everything in conformity with the purpose of his will, 12in order that we, who were the first to hope in Christ, might be for the praise of his glory. 13And you also were included in Christ when you heard the word of truth, the gospel of your salvation. Having believed, you were marked in him with a

33

seal, the promised Holy Spirit, [14]who is a deposit guaranteeing our inheritance until the redemption of those who are God's possession—to the praise of his glory.

God's Purposefulness

To many students of the Bible, the opening lines of Paul's letter to believers in Ephesus contain one of the strongest scriptural treatments on the doctrine of predestination (election). Even though the passage speaks with clarity to many believers, some take exception and call this view *predetermination.* One interpretation states that God planned and then carried out his plan. Another suggests that God made plans based on foreknowledge. Both views, however, acknowledge God's plans and purposes. In our passage from Ephesians it would be difficult for any of us not to see God's purposefulness.

In Ephesians 1:3 the apostle offers a stirring doxology and then goes on to explain what has elicited his praise. The conjunction "For" in 1:4 points to a choice God has made. The words "chose us" imply a conscious act of the will—God did this on purpose. The timing of God's choice further implies a plan. This was not a spur-of-the-moment decision; it was a well-thought-out plan drawn up "before the creation of the world" (1:4).

In the next sentence Paul uses the stronger word "predestined" (1:5). He also uses the word "us." Paul is talking about our destiny, preplanned in the mind of God. Then like a parenthetical phrase to give clarification, there's the clause "in accordance with his pleasure and will." This destiny that was being laid out for us was something God *wanted.* It conformed to God's will; it was in God's pleasure to prepare this destiny for us. In 1:11 we see the same terminology again: "chosen," "predestined," "according to the plan," "in conformity with the purpose of his will." The point could hardly be driven home much more emphatically.

What Did God Have In Mind?

What was God so intent upon making happen? The answer at first seems obvious: God chose us "to be holy and blameless" (1:4). But then Paul indicates that God had even more in mind: our destiny "in accordance with [God's] pleasure and will" was that we become like "sons" through the work of God's Son, Jesus Christ. In other words, God wanted to adopt us as children through Christ the Son, giving us full inheritance rights in the family of God (see Eph. 2:19-20). God so wanted us to be his children that he planned it before history, and in history God gave his own Son to complete the great plan of providing us "the right to become children of God" (John 1:12). (See also Rom. 8:12-17; Gal. 3:26-4:7.)

But why does God so desire children? The answer comes clear no less than three times in the brief paragraphs we are studying from Ephesians 1. In 1:6 Paul says God has done this "to the praise of his glorious grace." In 1:12 we see it again: "in order that we . . . might be for the praise of his glory." And in 1:14 we learn that we receive the "deposit" of the Holy Spirit as a guarantee of "our inheritance," thus showing that we are "God's possession—to the praise of his glory." As a part of all creation intended to proclaim the glory of God, we humans, the crown of creation, are intended to glorify the Creator. Our purpose is to praise God for "his glorious grace," for choosing us, and for "guaranteeing our inheritance."

Just as a tarnished creation groans with the inability to sing perfect praise to God, we cannot perfectly glorify God except as redeemed sons and daughters. So the bottom line is that God plans to bring us back into relationship with him so that we can give God the full glory we are intended to give. Salvation provided and received through Jesus Christ leads to praise, to heartfelt gratitude for all God has done. In fact, since salvation through Christ brings us in line with "the purpose" of God's "pleasure and will" (1:5, 11), it's impossible for us not to give God glory. And, again, this is glory that God has planned and purposed for us to give (see 2:8-10; see also Heidelberg Catechism, Q&A 64).

"Whatever You Do . . ."

At some time in your life you have probably received advice that began with the warning "Whatever you do . . ." For example, you might have been told,

- "Whatever you do, don't lose your ticket . . ."
- "Whatever you do, always look both ways . . ."
- "Whatever you do, keep your hands on the wheel . . ."
- "Whatever you do, be polite . . ."

Whether negative or positive, "Whatever you do . . ." instructions are often the most serious kind. Similarly, the apostle Paul wanted to convey with all seriousness the utter importance of giving glory to God. So in summarizing a discussion about Christian freedom he wrote: "Whether you eat or drink or whatever you do, do it all for the glory of God" (1 Cor. 10:31).

It was a fairly common difficulty for Corinthian believers to wonder what to do in some situations in which they interacted with unbelievers (in this case, it had to do with eating meat offered to idols). Paul gives some practical advice, but he also realizes that not all situations are equal and that few "rules" cover all possible bases. One principle, however, remains: "Whatever you do, do it all for the glory of God."

When we think about the vastness of God's creation and the "weightiness" of God's glory revealed in creation as well as in Scripture and in the Son of God himself (as we noted in lesson 3), we can see that Paul's "whatever" can apply generally to all contexts. As Jesus himself showed and as he also taught Peter, God can be glorified even in our death (John 21:19). Paul was well aware of this fact, as we can see from passages like 2 Corinthians 4:7-15 and Philippians 1:20-26 and 2:5-11. The principle of giving glory to God becomes the standard for all our actions and decisions.

What Do You Have In Mind?

Just as God was intentional and purposeful about creating and redeeming us, we have to be intentional and purposeful about glorifying God. Because we are still on our way toward becoming "mature, attaining to the whole measure of the fullness of Christ" (Eph. 4:13), we have to work at giving glory to God so that it becomes a good habit. And as we grow in giving glory, we'll gradually find that even our unconscious choices glorify God.

For example, the other day when I was driving on a wide city street, I automatically ("unconsciously") moved from the right lane to the left lane when I approached a red light. I found myself thinking, "Why did I do that?" Then I realized that without consciously choosing, I had changed lanes so that any cars behind me could take advantage of the right-turn-on-red option if they needed to. I was pleased, but not in a prideful way, because I acted out of caring for someone else. At one time that simple action would never have occurred to me, but God is maturing me. No one may have noticed, but I did something I think Jesus would have done, and God was glorified. Other examples we might think of may include being patient with a new clerk at the bank or grocery store, and not stereotyping someone because of the way they look or talk.

Unless we live in very isolated situations, we all face many conscious choices of right and wrong each day. Some are tough. They involve a cost—sometimes a high cost. But when we choose the way of holiness and blamelessness, we glorify God. When we unashamedly let others know the intentionality of our choices (though doing so may involve more cost), we glorify God even more. In all of this, by the power of the Spirit working in us, glorifying God becomes for us a state of mind.

GENERAL DISCUSSION

1. Does it seem out of character or egotistical for God to draw so much attention to himself and his glory? Why or why not?

2. Can God's glory be added to or increased? Explain.

3. Can God's glory be subtracted from or diminished? Explain.

4. Give one or two examples of how you "unconsciously" affirm or detract from God's glory.

5. What are some areas in your life in which you have to make decisions that glorify God to some degree? In what ways, if any, will your decision making be different now that you've reflected on God's glory as the purpose of your salvation?

SMALL GROUP SESSION IDEAS

Opening (5-10 minutes)

Pray/Worship—Open with prayer, asking the glorious God of salvation to guide your study of this lesson material. To add a worship element, you might like to read parts of Psalm 27 that mention God's praise and glory, or you could try a praise song based on that psalm, such as "The Lord Is My Light and My Salvation."

Follow-up from previous sessions—Take a few minutes to follow up on the Till Next Time goalsetting options or on Group Project ideas that you and others may have decided to do.

Going Through the Material (15-20 minutes)
As in other sessions, you may wish to read through the Scripture passages together before moving into your discussion time. You may also wish to read and review sections of the study-guide notes.

Discussing the Material (25-30 minutes)
As in previous sessions, the discussion questions follow in the order of the written comments in the study guide, so it's possible to blend in the discussion questions as you go through the material.

Till Next Time (5 minutes)
Here are some goalsetting exercises you might like to use to follow up on the material for this lesson (or you could come up with some ideas of your own):

• Keep a journal for a full day, listing all the ways in which you personally have glorified God. Also ask the Holy Spirit to help you evaluate at the end of the day by reflecting along these lines: *Are there any ways in which I neglected to glorify God? What could I have done differently?*

• Along with or in place of the one-day-journal exercise, make a list of what is not specifically "praiseworthy" in your life. Then select one or two items from the list and make specific plans for either eliminating or redeeming that thing in your life. Then, seeking guidance by the Spirit, put your plans into action.

Closing (5-10 minutes)
After a time of sharing concerns and praises, close with prayer. You may wish to include a time of silent, confessional prayer at this time as well. If the Spirit is leading any of you to offer prayers of (re)commitment, either silently or aloud, feel free to do so. These elements may make your closing a bit longer than usual, so you may want to give yourselves extra time for prayer.

What is Jesus'
main focus in
his work?

5

A Ministry of Glory

In a Nutshell

In this lesson we concentrate on Jesus' main focus in all of his work. As we do that, we learn again that we, as Jesus' followers, must focus mainly on God's glory. While we need to be careful not to skip over the importance of the Son's glory, we must note carefully the example he set for us. Jesus put God's glory first so that God's will could be done—and for us that meant salvation so that we too might glorify God forever.

> Praise the LORD, O my soul;
> > all my inmost being, praise his holy name.
> Praise the LORD, O my soul,
> > and forget not all his benefits—
> who forgives all your sins
> > and heals all your diseases,
> who redeems your life from the pit
> > and crowns you with love and compassion,
> who satisfies your desires with good things
> > so that your youth is renewed like the eagle's.
>
> —Psalm 103:1-5

John 12:23-28

23Jesus replied, "The hour has come for the Son of Man to be glorified. 24I tell you the truth, unless a kernel of wheat falls to the ground and dies, it remains only a single seed. But if it dies, it produces many seeds. 25The man who loves his life will lose it, while the man who hates his life in this world will keep it for eternal life. 26Whoever serves me must follow me; and where I am, my servant also will be. My Father will honor the one who serves me.

27"Now my heart is troubled, and what shall I say? 'Father, save me from this hour'? No, it was for this very reason I came to this hour. 28Father, glorify your name!"

Then a voice came from heaven, "I have glorified it, and will glorify it again."

John 17:1-9, 15-19

¹Jesus . . . looked toward heaven and prayed:

"Father, the time has come. Glorify your Son, that your Son may glorify you. ²For you granted him authority over all people that he might give eternal life to all those you have given him. ³Now this is eternal life: that they may know you, the only true God, and Jesus Christ, whom you have sent. ⁴I have brought you glory on earth by completing the work you gave me to do. ⁵And now, Father, glorify me in your presence with the glory I had with you before the world began.

⁶"I have revealed you to those whom you gave me out of the world. They were yours; you gave them to me and they have obeyed your word. ⁷Now they know that everything you have given me comes from you. ⁸For I gave them the words you gave me and they accepted them. They knew with certainty that I came from you, and they believed that you sent me. ⁹I pray for them. I am not praying for the world, but for those you have given me, for they are yours.

". . . ¹⁵My prayer is not that you take them out of the world but that you protect them from the evil one. ¹⁶They are not of the world, even as I am not of it. ¹⁷Sanctify them by the truth; your word is truth. ¹⁸As you sent me into the world, I have sent them into the world. ¹⁹For them I sanctify myself, that they too may be truly sanctified."

Completing the Work

In lesson 1 we took a sweeping, panoramic look at Christ's high-priestly prayer in John 17. We noted especially that this very intimate conversation of Jesus with his heavenly Father—the longest we have on record—focuses intently on glory. It speaks of the Father's glory, and the Son's, and even our own—given to us by Jesus, given to him by the Father.

While Christ's glory and even our glory may be important to the Father (what an amazing thought!), Jesus' primary focus was the Father's glory. One might respond to this observation by pointing out that Jesus' first petition in his prayer was "Glorify your Son." That's true, but as we can see, that's not the whole petition. There's a very important connector that explains why Jesus asked to be glorified: "[so] that your Son may glorify you" (17:1). As we saw in lesson 1, Jesus clearly associates the glory that he brings to the Father with the *completion of his work* assigned by the Father (17:4). And in lesson 4 we talked about the ultimate purpose of God's plan being more than our salvation. Even that great act of God, which made it possible for us sinners to be reconciled with the Father, was "for the praise of [God's] glory" (Eph. 1:12; see 1:6, 14).

As he hung dying on the cross, Jesus declared again that his work was "finished," and "with that, he bowed his head and gave up his spirit" (John 19:30). And we can see from his prayer in John 17 that Jesus was referring to much more than the end of his physical life and the intense suffering and spiritual separation from the Father that he'd had to endure. Jesus' earthly mission, the work that the Father had given him from before the creation of the world (Eph. 1:4), was completed. From then on, the process of humiliation was over, and Jesus was marching on to victory and glory.

Christ had clearly revealed the Father to the followers God had given him (17:6). That revelation was a part of his work. And with his work complete, he "gave up his spirit," dying on the cross for our sake and for the sake of God's glory. Then the next thing he did among us was to reveal his glory by rising from the grave with his own body transformed and glorified, showing that he was victorious over sin and death. Jesus' resurrection marked the beginning of his glory being recognized throughout the spiritual and earthly realms, and our participation in that resurrection allows us to share in his glory.

Christ's prayer thus prophetically recognizes the completion of his work and its results—the fulfillment of God's plan to bring salvation to all who are chosen "for the praise of his glory" (Eph. 1:12).

"The Hour Has Come"

Now let's back up about seven days. The context in which we read Jesus' words in John 12 is the event of the triumphal entry. All the people have been praising God (and Jesus), using words and quotations that are unmistakable references to the coming Messiah (see John 12:12-19).

In large part this celebration is a public reaction to the rapid and exciting spread of news about Lazarus of Bethany, whom Jesus has raised from the dead (12:17-18). The Pharisees, in turn, are getting quite upset with these developments (12:19). Then John indicates that at some point soon after the triumphal entry, some Greeks who have come to Jerusalem ask the apostle Philip if they can see Jesus (12:20-22). And in response to that request, Jesus speaks the words we find in John 12:23-28, one of our Scripture passages for this lesson.

In these words Jesus begins to talk about his death and declares that anyone who would claim to serve him must follow him. The implication is that they must follow him even into death, if necessary.

Jesus' invitation to follow him is not for the purpose of enjoying a Sabbath stroll or basking in the glory of the praises he received as he entered Jerusalem—though he does promise that the Father will honor those who serve him (12:26). The invitation is to share in what is now troubling Jesus' heart, even in the midst of praise and fanfare. Jesus has come to a definitive moment in his ministry. He has come to face his death. And he has a choice. "What shall I say?" he asks; "'Father, save me from this hour'? No, it was for this very reason I came to this hour" (12:27). Instead of opting out, Jesus chooses to glorify the Father. So, as a result, he chooses death.

At this point we might be tempted to say, *Just a minute, what does the Father's glory have to do with this?* And the answer is *Everything.* Jesus makes this clear when he declares resolutely what his mission is all about: "Father, glorify your name!" (12:28). And Jesus doesn't make this choice for his own glory— though he will, as a result, be glorified. Jesus knows that to glorify the Father, he must take the path of sacrifice "according to [God's] plan" and "in conformity with the purpose of his will" (Eph. 1:11). The Father then assures the Son that his obedience does glorify the Father's name: "I have glorified it, and will glorify it again" (John 12:28).

Our Work, Our Hour

As we think about Jesus' hour and his completed work, what are we to think of our own work and our own hour? Is our work also finished? Has our hour come?

While Jesus' earthly mission may be complete, the mission of his church is not. While he rules at the Father's right hand, both he and we are still at work. Christ works as one glorified, as the King of kings and Lord of lords. He intercedes and mediates with the Father on our behalf (Rom. 8:34; 1 Tim. 2:5; 1 John 2:1) as we work by the power of his Spirit in his church here on earth.

Jesus didn't pray that we could go to the Father with him. Rather, he specifically said, "My prayer is not that you take them out of the world but that you protect them from the evil one" (17:15). Earlier when Jesus washed his disciples' feet, he said he was giving them a model to follow (13:3-17). Like Jesus' disciples, we too are called to follow. And as we work, following the guidance of Christ, our hour is still upon us. Each day we have work to do to the glory of God, so in that sense each day we face *our hour.*

Sometimes we may lose sight of the larger picture by focusing on Jesus' great commission (Matt. 28:19-20) or the great commandment (22:36-40; see 25:34-40) as our main task. Other times we may focus on modeling Christ by preaching good news to the poor, proclaiming freedom, recovery, release, and the Lord's favor (Luke 4:18-19; Isa. 61:1-2). All of these objectives are important as part of Christ's strategy for opposing the gates of hell with his church (Matt. 16:18). But the *main objec-*

tive or purpose to which this battle is oriented is that the Father's name be glorified. It cannot be stated any more clearly than in the words of the apostle Paul: "Whether you eat or drink or whatever you do, do it all for the glory of God" (1 Cor. 10:31).

Jesus' ultimate purpose was never far from his mind. Even in the midst of the crowd shouting his praises, right in the vortex of prophetic fulfillment (see Ps. 118:24-27; Zech. 9:9), Jesus was focusing on the full picture, which included a prophecy about the suffering Servant's sacrifice (Isa. 52:13-53:12). In that sacrifice the victory would be won, and through the victory God would be glorified.

Similarly, through victory after victory, Christ's followers through the centuries have been his witnesses "to the ends of the earth" (Acts 1:8), and God has been glorified (John 12:28). Our Lord and King has given us an ongoing ministry of glory.

GENERAL DISCUSSION

1. Think about Jesus' actions, his teachings, and his death. How are all these related to God's glory?

2. Is Jesus' death sufficient to provide for our salvation? Explain. How do Jesus' resurrection and ascension fit into God's plan and relate to God's glory?

3. Have you ever been in a situation in which something wonderful was happening but you didn't fully enjoy it because you were focusing on something yet to come or you were looking at the "bigger picture"? Share your thoughts about it with the rest of the group. Does comparing that experience with Christ's prediction of his death after the triumphal entry help you better understand the situation Christ was in? Why or why not?

4. Have you come to your own "hour" in which you've had to make a difficult choice in relation to God's glory? Think of one or two examples you'd like to share. Did you recognize at the time that God's glory was at stake? Explain. If not, how might that recognition have affected your choice or decision making?

5. To help us as we remain in the world, Jesus asked the Father to protect us "from the evil one" (John 17:15). In what ways have you needed or felt that protection? Reflect on one or two examples that you'd like to share with the rest of the group.

SMALL GROUP SESSION IDEAS

Opening (5-10 minutes)

Prayer—As you open in prayer, thank God for Jesus' faithful obedience and finished work of salvation, by which we have eternal life. Pray for understanding and insight as you study the lesson material together, and ask the Lord to help you learn from Scripture and from each other, to God's glory.

Follow-up from previous sessions—Take a few minutes to follow up on the Till Next Time goalsetting options or on other activities that you and others may have decided to do.

Going Through the Material (15-20 minutes)

As in previous sessions, you may wish to read through the Scripture passages together before moving into your discussion time. You may also wish to read and review sections of the study-guide notes.

Discussing the Material (25-30 minutes)

As in previous sessions, the discussion questions follow in the order of the written commentary, so it's possible to blend in the discussion as you go through the material.

Till Next Time (5 minutes)

Here's a goalsetting idea you could try as a way to follow up on the material for this session (or, if you like, try an idea of your own):

- For two or three days jot down every conscious decision you make to choose a path (action, behavior, words, tone, and so on) that would glorify God. Also during that time (privately) keep track of decisions that have not been glorifying to God.

Closing and Prayer (5-10 minutes)

Share concerns, praises, and insights from this lesson that you wish to bring before the Lord in prayer. Then pray together, thanking God again for the awesome gift of salvation in Christ and asking the Lord to help each one of you stand faithfully as servants of Christ and to be mindful of glorifying God in all you do. Also ask the Lord to keep protecting you each day from the temptations and attacks of the evil one. Everyone may join in, as well, with items they'd like to pray about. Close, if you like, with a psalm of comfort and praise, such as Psalm 23 or 103 (used at the beginning of the material for this lesson).

*Glory is the
main reason
Satan is our
enemy.*

REVELATION 12

6

The Battle Over Glory

In a Nutshell

The focus of this lesson is on spiritual warfare. At first we might wonder what this has to do with studying God's glory. But the reality of spiritual warfare is at the center of the Christian life, and the battle is about glory. Satan attacks everything that reflects and bears God's glory—especially the church of Christ and individual Christians.

> A mighty fortress is our God,
> a bulwark never failing;
> our helper he, amid the flood
> of mortal ills prevailing.
> For still our ancient foe
> does seek to work us woe;
> his craft and power are great,
> and armed with cruel hate,
> on earth is not his equal.
>
> [God's] Word above all earthly powers—
> no thanks to them—abideth;
> the Spirit and the gifts are ours
> through him who with us sideth.
> Let goods and kindred go,
> this mortal life also;
> the body they may kill:
> God's truth abideth still;
> his kingdom is forever!
>
> —Martin Luther, 1529; tr. Frederick H.
> Hedge, 1852; based on Psalm 46

Revelation 12

¹A great and wondrous sign appeared in heaven: a woman clothed with the sun, with the moon under her feet and a crown of twelve stars on her head. ²She was pregnant and cried out in pain as she was about to give birth. ³Then another sign appeared in heaven: an enormous red dragon with seven heads and ten horns and seven crowns on his heads. ⁴His tail swept a third of the stars out of the sky and flung them to the earth. The dragon stood in front of the woman who was about to give birth, so that he might devour her child the moment it was born. ⁵She gave birth to a son, a male child, who will rule all the nations with an iron scepter. And her child was snatched up to God and to his throne. ⁶The woman fled into the desert to a place prepared for her by God, where she might be taken care of for 1,260 days.

⁷And there was war in heaven. Michael and his angels fought against the dragon, and the dragon and his angels fought back. ⁸But he was not strong enough, and they lost their place in heaven. ⁹The great dragon was hurled down—that ancient serpent called the devil, or Satan, who leads the whole world astray. He was hurled to the earth, and his angels with him.

¹⁰Then I heard a loud voice in heaven say:

"Now have come the salvation and
the power and the kingdom
of our God,
and the authority of his Christ.
For the accuser of our brothers,
who accuses them before our God
day and night,
has been hurled down.
¹¹They overcame him
by the blood of the Lamb
and by the word of their
testimony;
they did not love their lives so much
as to shrink from death.
¹²Therefore rejoice, you heavens
and you who dwell in them!
But woe to the earth and the sea,
because the devil has gone down
to you!
He is filled with fury,
because he knows that his time
is short."

¹³When the dragon saw that he had been hurled to the earth, he pursued the woman who had given birth to the male child. ¹⁴The woman was given the two wings of a great eagle, so that she might fly to the place prepared for her in the desert, where she would be taken care of for a time, times and half a time, out of the serpent's reach. ¹⁵Then from his mouth the serpent spewed water like a river, to overtake the woman and sweep her away with the torrent. ¹⁶But the earth helped the woman by opening its mouth and swallowing the river that the dragon had spewed out of his mouth. ¹⁷Then the dragon was enraged at the woman and went off to make war against the rest of her offspring—those who obey God's commandments and hold to the testimony of Jesus.

A Different Perspective

One of the purposes of this study is to help us gain perspective in looking at our day-to-day lives, to help us focus on *what life is all about.* It's a call to filter everything we do by asking, *Will this give glory to God?*

In Revelation 12 we gain an unusual perspective on the biblical narrative about redemption in Christ. We see what has happened "behind the scenes" in the heavenly realms. The passage gives us a unique look at the birth of Christ and of God's people. It's an angelic perspective on what Jesus may have been referring to when he said, "I saw Satan fall like lightning from heaven" (Luke 10:18). Having a proper understanding of this perspective can help us identify a very important aspect of life—something we often refer to today as spiritual warfare. It's what the apostle Paul was talking about when he urged the believers in Ephesus,

> Be strong in the Lord and in his mighty power. Put on the full armor of God so that you can take your stand against the devil's schemes. For our struggle is not against flesh and blood, but against the rulers, against the authorities, against the powers of this dark world and against the spiritual forces of evil in the heavenly realms.

> —Ephesians 6:10-12

As we read from Revelation 12, we need to take note that this is apocalyptic literature. Its purpose isn't to present detailed accuracy or chronological consistency. To make an impression, it lays out the main truth and the big picture with sometimes shocking imagery and symbolism. When Satan is depicted as "an enormous red dragon" whose tail sweeps "a third of the stars out of the sky" (Rev. 12:3-4), the intent isn't for us to believe in dragons or to look for a vast number of shootings stars. These pictures are given to help us recognize the reality of the danger and the ferocity with which Satan fights. They depict Satan's great power and evil intent in wanting to devour Christ and destroy his church (12:4, 17). "A third of the stars" probably symbolizes that a great many angels fall with Satan (see 12:9), indicating that he has a huge army to work with. It could also indicate that Satan is raging against nature, which "declares the glory of God" (Ps. 19:1). Note, however, that one-third is only a limited amount, a fraction indicating that God remains in control of the cosmos and still reigns supreme. (See the use of similar fractions and other finite numbers in Rev. 8-9.)

Why Satan Is Our Enemy

Many of us don't think about Satan very much. Believers in Christ will readily agree that Satan is our enemy because he is God's enemy. But how often do we think of Satan really having anything personally against us or having a cause for attacking us? After all, we are saved in Christ and safe in God's hands, "and the evil one cannot harm [us]" (1 John 5:18), so why should he bother? But if we think in terms of the "big picture" in which our lives play a part, we know we can't become complacent about Satan's interests in us (against us). The Scriptures give us several clear warnings about Satan's ongoing war against humanity, particularly against God's people.

What we need to understand first is Satan's *motive*. Even in a civil court of law, establishing a motive is a key element in demonstrating guilt. Then we can understand why we need to be wary of Satan's attacks and thus be mindful of and involved in spiritual warfare.

Scripture informs us of a battle between Satan and God. We have very little information about this event, and some of the passages about it—along with passages that may appear to be about it—can be interpreted in different ways and on different levels. Our passage for this lesson is one of the most clear, stating, "There was war in heaven" (Rev. 12:7). But this passage is also full of symbolism, being a description of a vision given to the apostle John, so even this passage is difficult to interpret in detail. Jesus' mention in Luke 10 about Satan's fall from heaven may also be a reference to the result of this battle—and yet from the context it's difficult to say for sure.

A couple of passages in the Old Testament, Isaiah 14:12-15 and Ezekiel 28:12-17, which are also sometimes interpreted symbolically, may give us additional insight into Satan's fall and pre-fall status. These passages, though, are admittedly obscure, since they refer specifically not to Satan but to the kings of Babylon and Tyre, respectively, six to eight hundred years before Christ. On the other hand, Babylon is often pictured symbolically in Scripture (along with other cities and nations) as the great "city of the world" representing all the world's wickedness (see Isa. 13-14; 21:9; Rev. 14:8; 16:19; 17:5-18:24; see also Isa. 24-25). So in a way we might interpret Isaiah 14 and Ezekiel 28 as including veiled references to Satan and to the beginnings of his evil influence in this world. These passages about the kings of Babylon and Tyre certainly are interesting:

> How you have fallen from heaven,
>   O morning star, son of the dawn!
> You have been cast down to the earth,
>   you who once laid low the nations!
> You said in your heart,
>   "I will ascend to heaven;
> I will raise my throne
>   above the stars of God;
> I will sit enthroned on the mount of assembly,
>   on the utmost heights of the sacred mountain.

I will ascend above the tops of the clouds;
    I will make myself like the Most High."
But you are brought down to the grave,
    to the depths of the pit.

—Isaiah 14:12-15

"You were the model of perfection,
    full of wisdom and perfect in beauty.
You were in Eden,
    the garden of God;
every precious stone adorned you:
    ruby, topaz and emerald,
chrysolite, onyx and jasper,
    sapphire, turquoise and beryl.
Your settings and mountings were made of gold;
    on the day you were created they were prepared.
You were anointed as a guardian cherub,
    for so I ordained you.
You were on the holy mount of God;
    you walked among the fiery stones.
You were blameless in your ways
    from the day you were created
    till wickedness was found in you.
Through your widespread trade
    you were filled with violence,
    and you sinned.
So I drove you in disgrace from the mount of God,
    and I expelled you, O guardian cherub,
    from among the fiery stones.
Your heart became proud
    on account of your beauty,
and you corrupted your wisdom
    because of your splendor.
So I threw you to the earth;
    I made a spectacle of you before kings."

—Ezekiel 28:12-17

While trying to avoid the trap of overspeculation, we can safely say that Satan once had great rank and power before the throne of God. And likely because he wanted more—that is, he wanted to "be like God" (see Gen. 3:5)—Satan and his followers (whom we would now refer to as fallen angels or demons) fought against God and the holy angels (Rev. 12:7). Satan's loss in this heavenly conflict resulted in his being "hurled down" to the earth along with his followers (12:9), apparently retaining his created power but having lost his glory. The battle was about power and glory.

Having failed, Satan lost his position and the great glory he once had. And now, like a raging dragon, he is bent on devouring us, who are favored with glory, being made in God's image. It's fair to say that Satan wouldn't want us to have any glory—after all, if he's lost his and can't have any, why should we? This gets at the root of Satan's motive for attacking us. It likely has to do with pride, envy, and vengeance.

For example, look at a parallel incident where a brother and sister are fighting over a toy. When their father intervenes and takes the toy away, the brother isn't overly concerned that the toy is taken away. He just wants to make sure that his sister doesn't get to play with the toy either!

Obsessed in his pride and envy, Satan has tried continually to destroy us as the crown of God's creation. But to no avail. When Satan succeeded in leading our first parents into sin, God promised to send a deliverer from among their descendants who would crush the serpent's head (Gen. 3:15; see Ps. 2; Rev. 12:5). And that's exactly what Jesus did, freeing us from the debt of sin and making new life possible for us (2 Cor. 5:17-21; Col. 2:13-15). Even now, knowing "that his time is short," Satan continues trying to destroy God's people (Rev. 12:12, 17). So as long as we are still susceptible to sin—and thus to distorting the reflection of God's glory in us—we do well to "be self-controlled and alert," knowing that our "enemy the devil prowls around like a roaring lion looking for someone to devour" (1 Pet. 5:8).

Because Satan has lost his glory, his only option for a "consolation prize" is to try to destroy God's glory and all that God has made to reflect and reveal his glory—creation, the Scriptures, Christ the Savior, and humanity (especially the people of God). And as we've been observing throughout this study, God has chosen us in Christ to be the primary agents of his glory.

To Top It Off

In lesson 1 we glanced at Christ's incredible statement that he intentionally shares his glory (which is also the Father's glory) with us (John 17:22). Paul describes us similarly as "co-heirs with Christ," explaining that one of the things we share with Christ is "his glory" (Rom. 8:17). In another passage Paul explains again—as in Ephesians 1 (see lesson 4)—that "from the beginning God chose [us] to be saved" and called us to this salvation through the gospel so that we might "share in the glory of our Lord Jesus Christ" (2 Thess. 2:14).

So we are not only *agents* but also *recipients* of God's glory, which Satan failed to get and thus wants to destroy—along with anything that reflects it. The picture of the battle in Revelation 12 represents, in some respects, an ongoing battle that's still being fought (see Rev. 12:12, 17). The battle is about God's glory, and we are called to the front lines of this battle. What's more, this battle is no mere skirmish. It is war, and it involves some of the heaviest fighting the heavens and earth have ever seen.

We are not to take this warfare lightly. We are not given the option of running away from it, and denial won't make it go away. When we purposely choose to give glory to God in all that we do and say, with all that we have and all that we are, Satan will take notice, and we will be targeted. That's why Paul instructs us on the nature of the battle, our defenses, and our weaponry (Eph. 6:10-18).

In response, we acknowledge that we are called to discernment and diligence. "On all occasions with all kinds of prayers and requests," we "pray in the Spirit" that we may "be strong in the Lord and in his mighty power" (6:10, 18). "In the Spirit" we know the importance and seriousness of giving glory to God.

GENERAL DISCUSSION

1. In what ways do you think Revelation 12 can help to enlighten our perspectives on other parts of Scripture? What does this passage reveal to us about the glory of God?

2. When you realize that giving glory to God makes you a potential target for attack, how does that make you feel? What are some practical ways in which you can put on the armor Paul describes in Ephesians 6:10-18?

3. Have you ever been under specific spiritual attack? Reflect on the circumstances, and work out a brief description of the situation. What happened? In what ways did you sense God working to help you? Share your thoughts with the rest of the group.

SMALL GROUP SESSION IDEAS

Opening (5-10 minutes)

Pray/Worship—Open with prayer, asking the sovereign Lord for insight and wisdom during this session as you discuss God's glory in the context of spiritual warfare. Singing a stanza or two of "A Mighty Fortress Is Our God," as printed at the beginning of this lesson, may be a fitting way to include a worship element at this time. Or you may wish to read from Psalm 46, on which that hymn is based. Other passages that can help us focus on God's comfort, strength, and glory in the midst of spiritual attacks are Numbers 6:24-26; Deuteronomy 33:26-39; Psalms 2-4; 121-122; 125-127; Isaiah 9:2-7; 11:1-10; 60:1-3.

Follow-up from previous sessions—Take a few minutes to follow up on the Till Next Time goals or on other activities you and others may have decided to do.

Going Through the Material (15-20 minutes)

Whatever approach you use for getting into the topic of spiritual warfare, be sure to spend most of your time and energy focusing on the heart of the issue—that is, on God's glory.

The following quotation from John Calvin lends significant historical credence to the church's position on the reality and seriousness of satanic and demonic influences:

> All that Scripture teaches concerning devils aims at arousing us to take precaution against their stratagems and contrivances, and also to make us equip ourselves with those weapons which are strong and powerful enough to vanquish these most powerful foes. For when Satan is called the god [2 Cor. 4:4] and prince [John 12:31] of this world, when he is spoken of as a strong armed man [Luke 11:21; cf. Matt. 12:29], the spirit who holds power over the air [Eph.

2:2], a roaring lion [1 Peter 5:8], these descriptions serve only to make us more cautious and watchful, and thus more prepared to take up the struggle. . . . We have been forewarned that an enemy relentlessly threatens us, an enemy who is the very embodiment of rash boldness, of military prowess, of crafty wiles, of untiring zeal and haste, of every conceivable weapon and of skill in the science of warfare. We must, then, bend our every effort to this goal: that we should not let ourselves be overwhelmed by carelessness or faintheartedness, but on the contrary, with courage rekindled stand our ground in combat. Since this military service ends only at death, let us urge ourselves to perseverance. Indeed, conscious of our weakness and ignorance, let us especially call upon God's help, relying upon him alone in whatever we attempt, since it is he alone who can supply us with counsel and strength, courage and armor.

. . . Moreover, in order that we may be aroused and exhorted all the more to carry this out, Scripture makes known that there are not one, not two, nor a few foes, but great armies, which wage war against us. . . .

The fact that the devil is everywhere called God's adversary and ours also ought to fire us to an unceasing struggle against him. For if we have God's glory at heart, as we should have, we ought with all our strength to contend against him who is trying to extinguish it. If we are minded to affirm Christ's Kingdom as we ought, we must wage irreconcilable war with him who is plotting its ruin. Again, if we care about our salvation at all, we ought to have neither peace nor truce with him who continually lays traps to destroy it. . . .

—*Institutes of the Christian Religion,* 1.14.13-15

Before moving into your discussion time, you may also wish to read Revelation 12 together and to review some of the comments in the study guide.

Discussing the Material (25-35 minutes)

As in previous sessions, the discussion questions follow in the order of the written commentary, so it's possible to blend in the discussion questions as you go through the material. Since there are only three General Discussion questions suggested for this session, you should have plenty of time to explore each one in detail.

Till Next Time (5 minutes)

Here's a goalsetting option you could try as a way to follow up on the material for this session (or you could try an idea of your own):

- Using a concordance or Bible dictionary, look up as many passages as you can find that give warnings to believers about Satan (the devil, the evil one) and his demons. Then look for passages that give assurance about the spiritual warfare we face—especially with regard to God's sovereignty and glory as well as God's care for us. Write out several of the more compelling passages on index cards, and commit yourself to memorizing those Scriptures throughout the coming weeks.

Closing (5-10 minutes)

Share concerns and praises, and then close with prayer, asking especially for God's wisdom and protection in dealing with any spiritual warfare issues you may have encountered during this session. You may want to build your closing prayer time around your discussion of General Discussion questions 2 and 3, praying specifically for each other to be equipped with the armor of truth, righteousness, peace, faith, salvation, knowledge of the Word, and prayer.

If you like singing, you could end with a hymn that encourages us to be mindful of God's victory and glory in spiritual warfare, such as "Onward Christian Soldiers," "For All the Saints," or "Christian, Do You Struggle."

Group Study Project (Optional)

If any of you are interested in gaining more insight and information on spiritual warfare, we recommend the following:

- *Victory over the Darkness: Realizing the Power of Your Identity in Christ* (Regal Books, 1990, 2000) by Neil T. Anderson.

- *The Bondage Breaker: Overcoming Negative Thoughts, Irrational Feelings, Habitual Sins* (Harvest House, 1990, 2000) by Neil T. Anderson.

- *Straight Talk About Spiritual Warfare: What the Bible Teaches, What You Need to Know* (CRC Publications, 1999) by Jeff Stam. An accompanying leader's guide (5 sessions) is available for group study. For more information or to order, call 1-800-333-8300 or visit **www.FaithAliveResources.org**.

What happens
to us when we
glorify God?

7

MATTHEW 5:1-14; GALATIANS 5:22-25; PHILIPPIANS 4:4-9; HEBREWS 13:15

Our Sacrifice of Praise

In a Nutshell

Let's look now at the progression that must take place as we seek to lead lives that glorify God. The progression begins with the transformation of our inner attitudes and moves on to the positive development of our outward actions displaying the fruit of the Spirit. As we "keep in step with the Spirit" working in us (Gal. 5:25), the result is spiritual growth and more and more glory given to God each step of the way.

> We bring the sacrifice of praise
> into the house of the Lord.
> We bring the sacrifice of praise
> into the house of the Lord.
>
> And we offer up to you
> the sacrifices of thanksgiving,
> and we offer up to you
> the sacrifices of praise.
>
> —Kirk Dearman. © 1984, John T. Benson
> Publishing Co., admin. Brentwood-Benson Music
> Publishing, Inc. Used by permission.

Matthew 5:1-14

¹Now when he saw the crowds, he went up on a mountainside and sat down. His disciples came to him, ²and he began to teach them, saying:

³"Blessed are the poor in spirit,
for theirs is the kingdom of heaven.
⁴Blessed are those who mourn,
for they will be comforted.
⁵Blessed are the meek,
for they will inherit the earth.
⁶Blessed are those who hunger and
thirst for righteousness,
for they will be filled.
⁷Blessed are the merciful,
for they will be shown mercy.
⁸Blessed are the pure in heart,
for they will see God.
⁹Blessed are the peacemakers,

for they will be called sons of God.
¹⁰Blessed are those who are persecuted
 because of righteousness,
for theirs is the kingdom of heaven.

¹¹"Blessed are you when people insult you, persecute you and falsely say all kinds of evil against you because of me. ¹²Rejoice and be glad, because great is your reward in heaven, for in the same way they persecuted the prophets who were before you.

¹³"You are the salt of the earth. But if the salt loses its saltiness, how can it be made salty again? It is no longer good for anything, except to be thrown out and trampled by men.

¹⁴"You are the light of the world. A city on a hill cannot be hidden."

Galatians 5:22-25

²². . . The fruit of the Spirit is love, joy, peace, patience, kindness, goodness, faithfulness, ²³gentleness and self-control. Against such things there is no law. ²⁴Those who belong to Christ Jesus have crucified the sinful nature with its passions and desires. ²⁵Since we live by the Spirit, let us keep in step with the Spirit.

Philippians 4:4-9

⁴Rejoice in the Lord always. I will say it again: Rejoice! ⁵Let your gentleness be evident to all. The Lord is near. ⁶Do not be anxious about anything, but in everything, by prayer and petition, with thanksgiving, present your requests to God. ⁷And the peace of God, which transcends all understanding, will guard your hearts and your minds in Christ Jesus.

⁸Finally . . . whatever is true, whatever is noble, whatever is right, whatever is pure, whatever is lovely, whatever is admirable— if anything is excellent or praiseworthy— think about such things. ⁹Whatever you have learned or received or heard from me, or seen in me—put it into practice. And the God of peace will be with you.

Hebrews 13:15

Through Jesus . . . let us continually offer to God a sacrifice of praise—the fruit of lips that confess his name.

Safety at Risk?

We are called to bring "a sacrifice of praise" before God (Heb. 13:15). From the perspective of lesson 6 we can see (perhaps in a new way for some of us) how praise can be related to sacrifice. Not only is our praise an offering to God, but it can also result in great personal cost in terms of spiritual warfare. As believers in Christ, who has opened the way for us to receive and reflect more and more of God's glory, our giving praise to God (glorifying God) opens us to the threat of more and more attacks from the enemy.

In lesson 4 we talked of our being created, chosen, and saved in order to praise and glorify God in all we do. Our sacrifice of praise becomes an inner motivation prompted by the Holy Spirit. It becomes almost instinctive, except that instinct is unlearned. Our sacrifice of praise is thought out and purposeful. As we walk more closely with God, "in step with the Spirit" (Gal. 5:25), God's desires more fully become the desires of our heart (see Ps. 37:3-6). Our thoughts and actions stem from the desires of our heart, which is being transformed more and more by the Holy Spirit (2 Cor. 3:18). We express our praise of

God inwardly, outwardly, and more and more "naturally" all the time. And while this growth in glorifying God makes us all the more annoying to the devil, we know by the power of the Spirit that "if God is for us," nothing can win against us; "neither death nor life, neither angels nor demons . . . nor any powers . . . will be able to separate us from the love of God that is in Christ Jesus our Lord" (Rom. 8:31, 38).

An Inner Attitude

Early in his teaching ministry Jesus delivered to his disciples and to many other listeners a body of teachings that has become known as the Sermon on the Mount (Matt. 5-7; see also Sermon on the Plain—Luke 6:17-49). Matthew's record of these teachings begins with what we often call the Beatitudes, or "blessings" (from the phrase *beati sunt,* "blessed are," in the Latin Vulgate; the original Greek for this phrase is *makarioi*). In these blessings Jesus is teaching about an inner pattern of thinking, an attitude that affects the core of our being. Those who live and walk in this attitude will be blessed, says Jesus. They will experience the blessedness of the kingdom of heaven.

Jesus is not simply giving a special benediction ("good word") to the downtrodden and suffering ("the poor in spirit" and "those who mourn"). While he does show compassion and calls us to help the needy, whatever those needs may be (see Matt. 4:23-25; 25:31-46), Jesus goes beyond that here. He is blessing believers whose spirits are not haughty or puffed up. These blessings stand in contrast with Jesus' later sharp criticism of religious leaders whom we might call "rich in spirit" (see Matt. 23). (Read *rich* here in the sense of worldly wealth and power and the pride they are based on. Look again at Isaiah 14 and Ezekiel 28 for comparisons with worldliness.)

When Jesus blesses those who mourn, for example, he is blessing their compassion, a display of their commitment to righteousness, which they have to have in order to sincerely grieve. We can stand with hurting people and love them through mutual grief over their personal loss. We can also mourn the loss of integrity and righteousness in a corrupt society. These are aspects of an inner attitude being shaped by the Holy Spirit. Gradually this attitude grows more and more to drive our thinking, our words, and our actions. And it's through our thinking, words, and actions that we give to or rob from the storehouse of God's glory.

With the attitude of righteousness planted firmly in our hearts, we are blessed and we can rejoice because we are building up a "reward in heaven" (Matt. 5:12). We are glorifying God as salt and light in this world (5:13-14), allowing people around us to taste and see the love of Jesus through us and the glory of God reflected in us.

An Outward Display

Just as Jesus listed blessing upon blessing for those with righteous, God-glorifying attitudes, Paul, in his letter to the churches in Galatia, lists many facets of the fruit of the Spirit. It should be noted, first of all, that the word for "fruit" in Galatians 5:22 is singular. "Love, joy, peace, patience, kindness, goodness, faithfulness, gentleness and self-control" should not be thought of as gifts of the Spirit, given in different measure, with one believer having one gift and another believer having another, as Paul explains in 1 Corinthians 12. In Galatians 5 Paul is calling us to bear the Spirit's "fruit," and all of the characteristics listed in Galatians 5:22-23 are facets of that fruit. We should not think in terms of picking and choosing the facets that best fit our own character or personality traits. We need to display them all. Nor should we assume that these facets of spiritual fruit represent an exhaustive list. Anything that produces a positive change in us and outwardly glorifies God represents spiritual fruit in our lives.

The fruit of the Spirit is our outward behavior as believers whom the Spirit of Christ is transforming. When we purposefully show love, we invite others to experience what Christlikeness tastes like. When we are faithful in our commitments and gentle in our relationships with others, when we show self-control in difficult situations, people cannot help seeing something different reflected in us. When they ask— and they will—what it is they are seeing, we can glorify God not only in displaying the Spirit's fruit but also by saying, *What you see in me is a result of the wonderful love of Christ and the rich blessing of God the Father. I'm being transformed inside and out by the Spirit of God, who now lives in me and makes it possible for me to bear fruit that glorifies God.*

Fruit is not optional. Biotic principles tell us that if an organism is not growing and bearing its intended fruit, it is sick, dying, or dead. Jesus explained it this way, saying: "I am the true vine, and my Father is the gardener. He cuts off every branch in me that bears no fruit, while every branch that does bear fruit he prunes so that it will be even more fruitful" (John 15:1-2). God wants to shape us so that we bear fruit, because that's one of the primary ways by which we glorify God. Later in the same discussion Jesus explains, "This is to my Father's glory, that you bear much fruit, showing yourselves to be my disciples" (15:8).

A New Focus

In another letter Paul gives several instructions to the believers in Philippi. He encourages them to rejoice—not just sometimes, but always (Phil. 4:4). Paul urges them also to be gentle in ways that are obvious to everyone (4:5). And they are not to "be anxious about anything" but, rather, to take everything to God in prayer (4:6). Then God's unfathomable peace (blessedness, *shalom*) will "guard" their hearts and minds "in Christ Jesus" (4:7). Sounds familiar, doesn't it? Paul is repeating instructions he has written earlier to the Christians in Galatia. He's saying, "Be fruitful." (Note also similarities to the advice Paul gives in Ephesians 6:10-18 on the armor of God.)

Then in Philippians 4:8 Paul gives a comprehensive wrap-up, saying that *anything* that fits into the categories of being true, noble, right, pure, lovely, and admirable—in sum, anything that is "excellent or praiseworthy"—is to be the focus of our attention.

Notice how these categories build on each other. Something might be true (*ruthless marketing and price-slashing can wipe out competition*) but not noble. Something may seem noble (*I should help him out by giving him some of my test answers*) but not be right. And so on. As the criteria peak, Paul sums up with "excellent or praiseworthy"—and here again we are reminded of giving glory (*praise*), which of course means glorifying God. What's more, we are not only to "think about such things" but also to take whatever we have learned and "put it into practice" (4:8-9).

Our lives are full of things and activities and even thoughts that are not necessarily bad. But Paul challenges us to reach higher, to strive for God's glory. *Look up, he's saying, not just to be good and moral, or to worship any old thing, or to gain glory for yourself, but to give sacrificially, to give wholly of yourself for God's glory.* What Paul is saying here is really a further explanation of his teaching in 1 Corinthians 10:31: "Whether you eat or drink or *whatever* you do, do it all for the glory of God."

GENERAL DISCUSSION

1. Read through the Beatitudes of Matthew 5 again. What aspect of a transformed inner attitude is Jesus getting at with each statement? List some practical examples for living out that attitude in your own life.

2. Think through the outer expressions that Paul describes as the fruit of the Spirit. List the facets of spiritual fruit that are evident in your life, and how. If not all of the facets are evident in some way, take note of behaviors in which you have fallen short. What can you do to make the fruit of the Spirit more evident in your life?

3. What events, positive or negative, has God been able to use in your life to increase (shape) your fruitfulness? What events, if any, have eaten away or destroyed some of your fruit?

4. What do you think of Paul's advice in Philippians 4:8-9? Does it seem too narrow or unrealistic? Explain. Have you fully dedicated yourself to living by the principles Paul is teaching here? If not, why not? How would your life be different if you lived that way?

SMALL GROUP SESSION IDEAS

It may be wise to spend some extra time in prayer as you prepare for this lesson. You may want to pray specifically about any needs for repentance and forgiveness (or forgiving) that any of you may have, since a number of issues along these lines may surface during your discussion.

Opening (5-10 minutes)

Pray/Worship—Open with a prayer asking God for discernment and courage as you reflect on inner attitudes and outward actions in relation to God's glory. You may also want to mention any prayer concerns that the lesson material may have brought to mind while you were preparing for this lesson.

If you like singing together, you could use the song printed at the beginning of the lesson material. Or you may find that another hymn such as "Blessed Jesus, at Your Word" would also be fitting.

Follow-up from previous sessions—Take a few minutes to follow up on the Till Next Time goalsetting options or on other activities that you and others may have decided to do.

Going Through the Material (15-20 minutes)

As in previous sessions, you may wish to read through the Scripture passages together before moving into your discussion time. You may also wish to read and review sections of the study-guide notes.

Discussing the Material (25-30 minutes)

Again, the discussion questions follow in the order of the written commentary in this study guide, so it's possible to blend in the discussion as you go through the material.

Till Next Time (5 minutes)

Look at your examples from your discussion of questions 1-3. Choose one or two areas that you know you need to work on, and develop a plan with specific goals to make those areas of your life more fruitful and God glorifying in the strength of the Holy Spirit.

Closing (5-10 minutes)

Any of you may mention praises and concerns (especially desires for change) that you would like to bring before the Lord in prayer. Remember also requests that you may have mentioned at the beginning of this session. In your closing prayer, ask God to help each one of you live in step with the Spirit as you grow in bearing fruit, being Christlike, and enjoying the blessedness of life in God's kingdom.

For a closing song, you could try a hymn such as "Lead Me, Guide Me" or "O Master, Let Me Walk with Thee."

*How's it all
going to turn
out?*

8

REVELATION 20:1-3, 10-11; 21:1-5, 22-26; 22:1-5

God's Glory Fully Revealed

In a Nutshell

The end of the book of Revelation gives us an inside look at the future. We get a glimpse of how history is going to turn out. This gift is for all believers. It's a vision of hope and assurance. It reminds us that God is faithful, that God's sovereignty will stand, and that God's glory will be fully revealed.

> You are worthy, you are worthy,
>   you are worthy, O Lord;
> you are worthy, to receive glory,
>   glory and honor and power:
> for you have created, have all things created,
>   for you have created all things,
> and by your pleasure they were created;
>   you are worthy, O Lord!

—Rev. 4:11; para. Pauline Michael Mills, 1963, alt.
© 1963, 1975, Fred Bock Music Co.
All rights reserved. Used by permission.

Revelation 20:1-3, 10-11

¹And I saw an angel coming down out of heaven, having the key to the Abyss and holding in his hand a great chain. ²He seized the dragon, that ancient serpent, who is the devil, or Satan, and bound him for a thousand years. ³He threw him into the Abyss, and locked and sealed it over him, to keep him from deceiving the nations anymore until the thousand years were ended. After that, he must be set free for a short time. . . .

¹⁰And the devil, who deceived them, was thrown into the lake of burning sulfur, where the beast and the false prophet had been thrown. They will be tormented day and night for ever and ever.

¹¹Then I saw a great white throne and him who was seated on it. Earth and sky fled from his presence, and there was no place for them. . . .

21:1-5, 22-26

¹Then I saw a new heaven and a new earth, for the first heaven and the first

earth had passed away, and there was no longer any sea. 2I saw the Holy City, the new Jerusalem, coming down out of heaven from God, prepared as a bride beautifully dressed for her husband. 3And I heard a loud voice from the throne saying, "Now the dwelling of God is with men, and he will live with them. They will be his people, and God himself will be with them and be their God. 4He will wipe every tear from their eyes. There will be no more death or mourning or crying or pain, for the old order of things has passed away."

5He who was seated on the throne said, "I am making everything new!" . . .

22I did not see a temple in the city, because the Lord God Almighty and the Lamb are its temple. 23The city does not need the sun or the moon to shine on it, for the glory of God gives it light, and the Lamb is its lamp. 24The nations will walk by its light, and the kings of the earth will bring their splendor into it. 25On no day will its gates ever be shut, for there will be no night there. 26The glory and honor of the nations will be brought into it.

22:1-5

1Then the angel showed me the river of the water of life, as clear as crystal, flowing from the throne of God and of the Lamb 2down the middle of the great street of the city. On each side of the river stood the tree of life, bearing twelve crops of fruit, yielding its fruit every month. And the leaves of the tree are for the healing of the nations. 3No longer will there be any curse. The throne of God and of the Lamb will be in the city, and his servants will serve him. 4They will see his face, and his name will be on their foreheads. 5There will be no more night. They will not need the light of a lamp or the light of the sun, for the Lord God will give them light. And they will reign for ever and ever.

Knowing the Ending

When reading a book, some people feel that they just have to know the ending before they're willing to read through the whole thing. Maybe they don't want to deal with an unexpected tragic outcome. Or perhaps they tend to get so involved in the story that they want to be sure everything is going to turn out okay.

In Revelation 20-22 we find out how the biblical drama of redemption is going to end. In this case, knowing the ending is *essential*. Our Lord tells us the ending to give us hope and assurance that Satan will be defeated, evil will be eliminated, and the glory of God will be revealed fully among us.

Step 1: Satan's Defeat

We are battling a defeated foe. In Revelation 12 we saw the dragon, "that ancient serpent called the devil" (Rev. 12:9), defeated and cast down to earth. In Genesis 3:15 God speaks of the woman's seed (Jesus) "crushing" that serpent's head. In Luke 10:18 Jesus ties the disciples' newly discovered authority over demons to Satan's fall from heaven. In Matthew 16:18 Jesus tells his disciples that the church will be founded on the Son of God and that Satan's kingdom will not be able to stand against the church's conquering, forward motion. Throughout the Gospels and Acts, Jesus and his apostles take charge over evil spirits. In Ephesians 1:20-21 Paul reminds us that the risen Christ is now seated at God's right hand as Lord above all rulers and authorities, powers and dominions. This is power and authority that God chooses to allow us to share (1:19; 2:6)! Satan's existence since his original heavenly battle against God (Rev. 12) has been a litany of defeat.

So why are we still in battle? Why is there spiritual warfare? Why do we and the church feel and act so defeated at times? These are appropriate questions. We often speak in terms of the "already, but not yet" in our Christian walk. We are already saved fully and freely by God's grace through Jesus Christ, and yet we are working out our salvation (Phil. 2:12) and God's kingdom has not yet fully come on this earth. Paul tells us that "our salvation is nearer now than when we first believed" (Rom. 13:11). We have been born again, and we have eternal life now, in present reality—and yet there is *so much more* to come. What has been completed at this point is Christ's death and resurrection—what it took to assure the final victory—but the battle is not over yet.

During World War II, the D-Day invasion of Normandy was seen as the turning point of victory for the Allied Forces, just as the battle of Gettysburg was seen as the turning point during the Civil War in the United States. These events were bloody, many lives were lost, and much fighting continued in both of these wars before they finally ended. Still, the outcome, the victory, had been assured in each case.

The same is true of the war between God (armed with the heavenly angels and the church of Christ) and Satan (armed with his fallen angels and all his influence over the world). The victory has been determined, but we are still in the final days of battle.

We must fight gloriously for the glory of God. James tells us that we do this by continued submission to God and by resisting (pushing back) the devil and his forces (James 4:7). Paul teaches that we must "put on the full armor of God" (Eph. 6:11). And John teaches that we must discern "the spirit of the antichrist" in the ongoing battle against evil. In the meantime, though, we are assured of victory "because the one who is in [us]"—Christ— is "greater than the one who is in the world"—Satan (1 John 4:3-4). As we literally live out the final chapter of redemption history, we give glory to God by recognizing the power of Christ in us and by actively joining in the defeat of Satan.

Step 2: God's Presence Among Us

Revelation 21 opens with the arrival of God. John sees the New Jerusalem coming, and he hears "a loud voice from the throne saying, 'Now the dwelling of God is with men, and he will live with them. They will be his people, and God himself will be with them and be their God'" (Rev. 21:3). Once again, but even more so than before, we can shout, "Immanuel, 'God with us'!" This picture is reminiscent of the Exodus accounts of God's glory coming upon Mount Sinai and filling the tabernacle, God's visible Presence with his people (see lesson 2).

As in the days of Moses, so too in the new Jerusalem—God's presence among his people shows clearly that, yes, these are God's people and that the Lord of heaven and earth is their God (21:3). This is God's covenant fulfilled; this is God's plan completed. The language here is no accident. It would immediately have reminded John of God's covenant to Abraham in Genesis 17:7: "I will establish my covenant as an everlasting covenant between me and you and your descendants after you for the generations to come, to be your God and the God of your descendants after you." And every believer knows, as Paul puts it, that "if you belong to Christ, then you are Abraham's seed, and heirs according to the promise" (Gal. 3:29).

In his presence among us, which cannot be experienced apart from his glory, God announces to the world, "These are mine, and I am theirs." And the more we glorify God now, the more magnificent will be the moment when God renews heaven and earth and comes to live among us in the fullness of his glory.

Step 3: God's Glory Fully Known

Even though the fullness of God dwells in Jesus Christ (Col. 1:19) and we experience aspects of that fullness even now (see 2 Cor. 1; Eph. 1:18-23; 2:6-10), we will experience in a fuller sense the glory of the triune God when all things are perfected and God lives among us. The real glory John sees in his vision—and, remember, he sees only a glimpse—is not in the removal of death, mourning, crying, or pain (21:4). Nor is the real glory found in the river of life, the streets of gold, the gates of pearl, the walls of precious gems, or the trees bearing a different crop of fruit every month (22:1-2). Nor is it found in the glory of the nations brought as an offering (21:26). The real glory is found in God.

The New Jerusalem is a city that will experience no night and need no light because the glory of God will be its light

(21:23; 22:5). "The throne of God and of the Lamb" will be there (22:3), and we will look on the brilliance of glory reflected in their faces and see as we've never seen before.

As I get older, I realize that I need more and more light to see, but some types of light are too brilliant, too harsh; they need to be reflected off a secondary source. The glory of God will be brilliant, but it won't be harsh. It will no longer have to be reflected off symbols or types or imperfect Christians. The light of God's glory will be purely seen from its one and only source. As the apostle Paul puts it, "Now we see but a poor reflection as in a mirror; then we shall see face to face. Now I know in part; then I shall know fully, even as I am fully known" (1 Cor. 13:12).

On that day Jesus' requests for us in John 17 will be fully fulfilled. Remember what he prayed? "Father, I want those you have given me to be with me where I am, and to see my glory, the glory you have given me. . . . I have made you known to them, and will continue to make you known in order that the love you have for me may be in them and that I myself may be in them" (17:24-26). "This is eternal life: that they may know you, the only true God, and Jesus Christ" (17:3).

GENERAL DISCUSSION

1. In what ways does it sometimes seem that Satan is far from defeated in our personal lives, in the church, and in the world? Give one or two examples from each of these areas.

2. What are some ways in which you and/or your church can more actively resist the devil? In what ways have you seen the devil flee?

3. Have you ever experienced God's presence in a unique or special way? What was it like? What response did it create in you?

4. In the past when you've thought about heaven, did your thoughts focus on experiencing God's glory firsthand? If so, how did you picture that experience? If not, why do you suppose you didn't?

SMALL GROUP SESSION IDEAS

Opening (5-10 minutes)

Pray/Worship—Open your session in prayer, asking that God's glory may be revealed to each of you in a special way as you study from the closing chapters of Revelation. You may also want to pray through a psalm that helps us focus on God's praise and glory, such as Psalm 57 or Psalm 72.

If you like singing, you could join together in the praise chorus "You Are Worthy," printed near the beginning of the notes for this session.

Follow-up from previous sessions—Take a few minutes to follow up on the Till Next Time goalsetting options or on other activities you and others may have decided to do.

Going Through the Material (15-20 minutes)

You may wish to read through the passages from Revelation together before moving into your discussion time. Since these chapters are so interesting in their entirety, you could also, of course, read them directly from your Bibles. Most Bibles divide these chapters into about six sections, so you could easily take turns by having each person read a section or a few paragraphs. You may also wish to read and review sections of the study-guide notes.

Discussing the Material (25-35 minutes)

The discussion questions follow in the same order as the sections of the study-guide notes, so you have the option of going through the questions as you work through the study-guide comments, if you like. Questions 1 and 2 relate to the section "Step 1: Satan's Defeat." Questions 3 and 4 correspond to the next two sections, respectively.

Till Next Time (5 minutes)

Here's a goalsetting option you could try as a way to follow up on the material for this session (or you could try an idea of your own):

- After spending some time in quiet, reflective prayer in which you listen carefully for God's Spirit to speak to your heart, draw or write your impressions of what heaven will be like. Whatever imagery or word pictures you use, try to keep the focus on God's living with us and on God's glory being fully revealed.

Closing (5-10 minutes)

Share prayer concerns and praises with each other. You may wish to mention issues that may have surfaced during your discussion time. In your closing prayer, ask that God's glorious presence may fill you more and more each day, enabling you to resist the devil and to glorify God more and more fully.

For a closing song, you could try, again, the praise chorus printed near the beginning of the notes for this session, or you could sing a doxology such as "To God Be the Glory" or "Glorify Your Name."

*We need to put
God's glory
into practice.*

9

ROMANS 11:33-36; REVELATION 4:8, 11

Doxology in All of Life

In a Nutshell

As we conclude our study on God's glory, it's important that we close not on a theoretical note but with some concrete ideas about putting the glory of God into practice. So this final lesson addresses three practical questions: *What is doxology? When do we give it?* and *How do we give it?*

> "Amen!
> Praise and glory
> and wisdom and thanks and honor
> and power and strength
> be to our God for ever and ever.
> Amen!"
>
> —Revelation 7:12

Romans 11:33-36

33Oh, the depth of the riches of the
  wisdom and knowledge of God!
  How unsearchable his judgments,
  and his paths beyond tracing out!
34"Who has known the mind of the Lord?
  Or who has been his counselor?"
35"Who has ever given to God,
  that God should repay him?"
36For from him and through him and
  to him are all things.
  To him be the glory forever! Amen.

Revelation 4:8, 11

8. . . "Holy, holy, holy
  is the Lord God Almighty,
  who was, and is, and is to come." . . .

11"You are worthy, our Lord and God,
  to receive glory and honor and
    power,
for you created all things,
  and by your will they were created
  and have their being."

Songs of Praise

Most of us don't picture the apostle Paul as an overly emotional type of guy. He was very studious and very serious, willing to die for what he believed. He didn't have the time (or perhaps the opportunity) for a wife and family, though he does indicate a longing for companionship (see Rom. 15:23-24)—but that may well have been so he could have an in-depth theological discussion with old friends. No, Paul doesn't seem the sort who might, for example, sing with abandon in the shower.

In a sense, though, that's exactly what Paul does in the closing verses of Romans 11—he pauses and lets loose with praise! It's as if he can no longer simply write about what God has done, communicating from his sharp mind; he has to belt it out from the heart. The result is one of the most extraordinary doxologies we find in Scripture.

In Revelation 4 we find two other beautiful doxologies. In John's vision of the throne of God in heaven we see four incredible creatures positioned around the throne. They never stop declaring God's holiness and eternity. Joining them in praise are twenty-four elders, who most likely represent the twelve tribes of Israel and the twelve apostles of Christ, who form the foundation of the church. Together they represent all of God's people, the ones chosen "before the creation of the world . . . in accordance with [God's] pleasure and will—to the praise of his glorious grace" (Eph. 1:4-6). Laying their golden crowns before the throne, they sing a stirring doxology to the Lord God, the Creator of all things.

What Is Doxology?

The word *doxology* comes from two Greek words that are used in one form or another more than 250 times in the New Testament. The first is the word *doxa* (also often used in the form *doxazo*), which is most commonly translated as "glory," "glorious," "glorified," or "praise." Other translations, depending on the context, are "splendor," "majesty," and, on at least one occasion, "celestial" (2 Pet. 2:10). The second word, *eulogia,* from which we derive the word *eulogy,* occurs less often than *doxa* and is most often translated as "praise," sometimes as "blessing," and one time each as "thanksgiving," "generous gift," and even "flattery." So a doxology is an expression of praise and glory. It recognizes splendor and majesty and can be given in the form of blessing, thanksgiving, or even appropriate flattery.

In Paul's doxology in Romans 11 the actual word for "glory" (*doxa*) occurs only at the very end: "To him be the glory forever!" (Rom. 11:36). But everything preceding it is also praise. Proclaiming the depth and richness of God's wisdom, the wonder of God's judgment and plans, the fact that God has no need of a counselor and is indebted to no one, and, as well, that all things exist in and through God, Paul is *eulogizing* God. The apostle is giving God glory through his praise.

The four creatures around the throne in Revelation 4 are simply stating facts. They are glorifying God by proclaiming God's uniqueness. The Lord God alone is holy, and only God has no beginning and no end. No part of creation can make this claim. God is totally other. This form of doxology sets God apart, lifting the Lord Almighty on high. The twenty-four elders have wrapped their doxology in a gift: their crowns— given to them by God, of course, in the first place. Their crowns represent their power, prestige, riches, and identity. The elders thus proclaim God's inestimable worth, focusing as the four creatures do on the simple fact of God's uniqueness and position—God alone is sovereign and creator.

When Do We Give It?

Considering all that God is and has done—around us, in us, for us, and through us—we have much on which to base our doxology to the Almighty. *And when do we give doxology to God?*

The four living creatures "never stop saying: Holy, holy, holy . . ." (Rev. 4:8). They are in a constant state of doxology. The elders follow the lead of the four creatures, building on their praise by declaring God's supremacy (4:9-10). While writing one of his most in-depth and complex theological treatises for the church, the apostle Paul stops right in the middle of what he's doing—and praises God. Why? Because at that moment the Spirit apparently poked Paul's heart and said, "Praise!"

If asked, many of us would say that the doxology we give to God is a formal response as part of a formal worship service. In many worship traditions there's a set time and place in the service for a doxological response. Somehow this doesn't seem to be the same as the response of the twenty-four elders or of Paul.

Just as Paul instructs us to "pray continually" (ever in an attitude of fellowship with God—1 Thess. 5:17), so we are always to be in an attitude of praise. In a worship service we are told when to pray, but we know there are also other times when we must pray. So too, while there are times in formal worship when we are prompted to respond in doxology, we should know there are also other times (always) when we can eulogize God with praise.

Just as prayer is intended to be spontaneous and natural, so is our praise of God. We should glorify God whenever we feel the urge, and we should feel the urge often. Whenever the goodness, the holiness, the uniqueness, the majesty, the love of God confront our minds and hearts, we should respond in doxology.

How Do We Give It?

The ways in which we can praise and glorify God are as many as the sands on the seashore. Paul preached, discipled, encouraged, admonished, and kept in touch by writing to his dear friends in Christ. The four living creatures stand respectfully around God's throne and speak God's praise. The twenty-four elders lay down their crowns as an offering to God's worthiness "to receive glory and honor and power" (Rev. 4:11). "Ten thousand times ten thousand" angels sing (5:11). David fought God's enemies, ruled as king, danced "with all his might" (2 Sam. 6:14), wrote psalms, and played his harp. Priests blew ram's horns, raised their hands, and served in the Lord's temple day and night (Ps. 134:1-2; 135:1-2). All of these are expressions of praise and glory.

Many of us have gifts or talents we can use to glorify God. We might sing or play an instrument during a worship service. We might also do the same when we're alone except for an appreciative audience of One—the Almighty. No matter where we are, we can offer doxology to God, as long as that's our intent. In our work, in our play, in all "we think, say, and do," we can "direct all our living," with the Spirit's help, so that God's name is "always honored and praised" (Heidelberg Catechism, Q&A 122).

We may need to eliminate pride from what we do. We may need to remove unholiness from our music and other art forms. We may need to abandon falsehood in our religious ceremonies. We may need to claim back much of what Satan has stolen and tainted, but the whole earth and all its glory belongs to God. Everything in it can be redeemed and used as a platform of doxology to the Lord God Almighty.

GENERAL DISCUSSION

1. What forms of doxology are used in formal worship in your church? Do certain forms of praise make you uncomfortable? If so, what are they, and what is disquieting to you about them?

2. What forms of informal worship do you participate in (individually and in a small group setting)? How do you praise God in those settings? In what ways, if any, is your praise different from the praise you give in formal worship?

3. Do some thinking about your talents and interests. In what ways do you praise and glorify God with these? In what ways do you think you could give God even more praise and glory through your talents and interests? As you reflect, ask the Spirit to help you stretch to come up with ideas you haven't thought of before.

4. After praying and reflecting for a few minutes, make a list, using brief descriptions, of things that you now realize you've never praised God for or about.

SMALL GROUP SESSION IDEAS

Extended praise time—As a part of this final lesson on God's glory, you may wish to spend an extended time in praise, if possible, either at the beginning or at the end of your session.

As we noted earlier, this lesson is intended to be very practical. Perhaps the whole lesson can become a purposeful exercise in giving glory to God.

Opening (5-10 minutes)

Pray/Worship—Open in prayer, dedicating your time together as an offering to God. Ask the Lord to bless each of you in such a way that it moves you to praise and glorify God.

To add a worship element at this time, you could join together in an extended praise time, as suggested above, or you could simply sing one or two songs of praise based on passages in Revelation 4, 7, or 11. Another option would be to read or pray through a praise psalm such as Psalm 96, 98, or 103.

Follow-up from previous sessions—Again, take a few minutes to follow up on the Till Next Time goalsetting options or on other activities you and others may have decided to do.

Going Through the Material (15-20 minutes)

As in previous sessions, you may wish to read through the Scripture passages together before moving into your discussion time. You may also wish to read and review sections of the study-guide notes.

Discussing the Material (25-30 minutes)

Again, the discussion questions follow in the order of the written comments in the study guide, so it's possible to blend in the discussion as you go through the material.

Post-Study Follow-Up (5 minutes)

Here are some goalsetting ideas that can help you to continue focusing on God's glory after finishing this Bible study:

- Memorize and meditate every day for a week on Paul's benediction in Ephesians 3:20-21. Incorporate this exercise into your daily devotions and prayers as often as you like. Think of ways in which God has responded to you beyond your asking or imagining, and purposefully give God glory for everything the Spirit in you brings to mind.

- As a follow-up to memorizing and meditating on Ephesians 3:20-21, do the same with other passages (or portions of them) that help you focus on God's amazing, glorifying work in your life, such as

  —Romans 8:18-39
  —1 Corinthians 15:55-58
  —2 Corinthians 3:17-18
  —2 Peter 1:5-8
  —any of Psalms 145-150
  —any other Scriptures mentioned in this study

  Use a concordance to find other passages that can help you focus on *praise* and *glory*. The point is to continue giving glory to God every day in all you do. Grow in the Lord and see what glorious things God can do through you!

Closing (5-10 minutes)

You may want to read Ephesians 3:20-21 as a benediction before or after your closing prayer. As usual, everyone may mention concerns and praises, especially in connection with the lesson material. Challenge yourselves also to follow up by using the goalsetting options described above (or by using ideas of your own in line with the Spirit's leading).

Close in prayer, asking God to fill each one of you with glory, to make you more Christlike by the power of the Holy Spirit living in you, and to help you put the praise and glory of God into practice in your lives. Everyone also may join in with prayer requests and praises. Thank God also for the hope we have in Christ—that our Lord will bring us into glory-filled life forever in his presence when he comes again.

You may wish to incorporate an extended praise time, as suggested above, or to close with a reading that helps you focus on God's glory. For example, the following lines from Q&A 122 of the Heidelberg Catechism could provide a fitting conclusion to this study:

> Help us to really know you, [Lord,]
> to bless, worship, and praise you
>   for all your works
>   and for all that shines forth from them:
>   your almighty power, wisdom, kindness,
>   justice, mercy, and truth.
>
> And . . .
>
> Help us to direct all our living—
>   what we think, say, and do—
> so that your name will never be blasphemed
>   because of us
> but always honored and praised.

Evaluation

Background

Size of group:
- ☐ fewer than 5 persons
- ☐ 5-10
- ☐ 10-15
- ☐ more than 15

Age of participants:
- ☐ 20-30
- ☐ 31-45
- ☐ 46-60
- ☐ 61-75 or above

Length of group sessions:
- ☐ under 60 minutes
- ☐ 60-75 minutes
- ☐ 75-90 minutes
- ☐ 90-120 minutes or more

Please check items that describe you:
- ☐ male
- ☐ female
- ☐ ordained or professional church staff person
- ☐ elder or deacon
- ☐ professional teacher
- ☐ church school or catechism teacher (three or more years' experience)
- ☐ trained small group leader

Study Guide and Group Process

Please check items that describe the material in the study guide:
- ☐ varied
- ☐ monotonous
- ☐ creative
- ☐ dull
- ☐ clear
- ☐ unclear
- ☐ interesting to participants
- ☐ uninteresting to participants
- ☐ too much
- ☐ too little
- ☐ helpful, stimulating
- ☐ not helpful or stimulating
- ☐ overly complex, long
- ☐ appropriate level of difficulty

Please check items that describe the group sessions:
- ☐ lively
- ☐ dull
- ☐ dominated by leader
- ☐ involved most participants
- ☐ relevant to lives of participants
- ☐ irrelevant to lives of participants
- ☐ worthwhile
- ☐ not worthwhile

In general I would rate this material as
☐ excellent
☐ very good
☐ good
☐ fair
☐ poor

Additional comments on any aspect of this Bible study:

Name (optional): _____

Church: _____

_____

City/State/Province: _____

_____

Please send completed form to

Word Alive / God's Glory
Faith Alive Christian Resources
2850 Kalamazoo Ave. SE
Grand Rapids, MI 49560

Thank you!